The See-Saw

Julia Hobsbawm is a mum, stepmum, wife, daughter, daughter-in-law, sister, sister-in-law, auntie, friend and businesswoman.

And the seasons, they go round and round
And the painted ponies go up and down
We're captive on the carousel of time.
We can't return, we can only look behind
From where we came
And go round and round and round
In the circle game.

'The Circle Game', Joni Mitchell

The See-Saw

100 Ideas for Work–Life Balance

JULIA HOBSBAWM

Atlantic Books
London

Published in Great Britain in 2009 by Atlantic Books,
an imprint of Grove Atlantic Ltd.

1 2 3 4 5 6 7 8 9

A CIP catalogue record for this book is available from the British Library.

ISBN: 978 1 84354 911 6

Printed in the UK by CPI Bookmarque, Croydon, CR0 4TD

Design by five twentyfive

Illustrations by Streeten Illustration © Nicola Streeten, 2009

Atlantic Books
An imprint of Grove Atlantic Ltd
Ormond House
26–27 Boswell Street
London
WC1N 3JZ

www.atlantic-books.co.uk

*In memory of Gretl Lenz, who was always
an inspiration to me.*

Contents

1. Superwoman Lands with a Bump
(and Superman Stops Flying Off)   1

2. See-Saw Cissies   17

   On the See-Saw: Shirley   27

3. The Thirty-Six-Hour Day   29

4. Little Angels and Devils   45

5. Damned by the 'Dammy'   73

   On the See-Saw: David   81

6. Work and Childcare on the See-Saw   85

7. The F-Word: Flexibility   99

   On the See-Saw: Amanda   112

8. Fitness Freaking Out   117

9. Me-Time (and the Non-Book Book Group)   123

   On the See-Saw: Sarah   137

10. Guilt: The G-Spot You Can Always Find   141

11. See-Saw Romance   151

   On the See-Saw: Linda   161

Afterword   163

Acknowledgements   168

Top Ten Headaches

The See-Saw gives us all headaches. My top ten are:

1. The **pressure** to work hard, play hard, and look your best all the time.
2. The fact that **modern living** takes up as much time as it saves (we've all felt this when stuck in call-centre hell).
3. Those **contradictory cultures** of parenthood, which urge us to work or yet also to stay at home for risk of damaging our children forever by fielding them out to nurseries and nannies.
4. The **lack of universal childcare or government recognition of carers** in any meaningful way, which ratchets up the pressure.
5. The fact that the work culture remains fixated by office-based, **nine-to-five rules**, which play havoc with any other competing demands. We are a long way from truly flexible working.
6. **Inequality in pay**, which makes women's lives even harder than men's (which aren't easy either).
7. The steep rise of the **cost of living**, which means that many of us are outpriced from our own lives.
8. The reality that **most households require two incomes** just to get by, even though increasingly there is often only one bread winner in the house working their socks off.
9. **School holidays and term-time schedules**, which are completely at odds with a largely inflexible workplace.
10. **The Always-On society** that never sleeps, so we very rarely say 'nighty night' to each other and conk out nice and early.

1

Superwoman Lands with a Bump (and Superman Stops Flying Off)

Overloaded is the New Overweight

I bet you hate this book already. I bet you think it confirms that (a) you need work–life balance and don't have it, and (b) you aren't getting enough of a balance because you are *doing it wrong*. If this was a diet book (and I have picked up plenty in my time), at this point you'd be wishing something would change about the way you eat, or think about food. You'd be longing somewhere, however secretly, for transformation.

Well, something *is* wrong: somewhere along the line not many of us are achieving great work–life balance. Or we worry that we aren't. Only children say, 'I'm bored,' because adults don't have time to be bored these days. They might say, 'I'm stressed,' but who has time to be bored? Overloaded is the new Overweight.

1

Everlasting Overload

I don't know about you, but I think about work–life balance a lot. I have to. If my life were a household budget I'd be down to zero every month at best, overdrawn every week at worst.

I relish being multiple things: mother, stepmother, wife, sister, daughter, daughter-in-law, auntie, great-auntie, colleague, and, of course, friend. My parents, my two brothers and I are close, and my cousins are like sisters. My life is not quite *The Waltons* – though I loved every minute of that 1970s American TV serial about a family where all the grandparents and their children and grandchildren live together and call out 'Goodnight' to each other – but we are all in each other's lives a good deal. Being close in family or business is a commitment that takes time, and no matter how enjoyable that is, it can often make you feel like an egg-timer on its last few seconds of sand.

Our children range in age from three to eighteen. Two of them are my husband's, and three of them are mine and his together. The job-that-never-ends called parenthood includes, of course, organizing school runs, play dates, assemblies, parents' evenings, homework, TV policing, settling sibling rivalry scores, reading, playing, talking, drum lessons, and fresh air enforcement. In return for this continuous work, we get the wonder of parenthood: being around several delightful, small and not so big people who are interesting, loving, and maddening in equal measure. Children amuse us and love us. And they scare the pants off us when they (a) scale down from the balcony aged nine, (b) insist on getting out of the bath unaided aged three and slip, or (c) don't return a mobile phone call aged fifteen at midnight on a Saturday.

 TOP TIP

Pause for breath and pause for thought instead of mindlessly rushing around.

Keeping the Show on the Road

My day work seems, by comparison, less stressful and more predictable, although technically it is hard to see where the 'day' of the job ends. I created and nurtured my business like a child. I shared its growing pains and take enormous pride in every new development. My team is like family, and my board are quite like brothers. Business families certainly fall somewhere in between strangers, friends, and siblings. I spend as much time with them in person and by email as with my own flesh and blood. In order to keep the various shows on the road, and because I'm in my mid-forties, I need to spend time I'd rather not have to spend, keeping the mid-life sag and tiredness levels fractionally at bay. This involves as little exercise as I can get away with, as much retail therapy as I can justify for clothes and make-up to make me look un-saggy generally, as well as to hide the eye bags, and reasonably close attention to haircuts, highlights, and, last but by no means least, manicures. It nearly kills me to sit still for the time it takes for them to dry and I always think I should be doing 'something else', but needs must and, to coin a well-known phrase, I'm worth it.

Rush Hour

Fantasy Me is someone who glides and doesn't rush, who gets to the end of her To Do List with a flourishing tick at the end of each day and has the energy to focus fully on the loved offspring her non-stressed gaze alights upon (that's before she plans world domination in business and after she has

TOP TIP

Make a meaningful To Do List, not a bottomless one.

TOP TIP

Ditch uneccessary work meetings. Have 'Telephone Tea' or perfect other techniques to have you home and connecting to your non-work life .

made her husband glad as glad can be that she is home). Fantasy Me knows where everything is at any given time, because everything has a neat place and is not in a disordered heap somewhere. Fantasy Me is, well, a fantasy. The truth is distinctly more chaotic than I dare admit.

And of course the truth hurts. There I am, often running around like a headless chicken who has missed a deadline, desperately going between board meetings and trying to organise dentist appointments and play dates (while knowing deep down that I can't remember the names of all my children's teachers or friends.) I want to rename parents' evening parents' afternoon and find myself bitterly resenting that the latest appointment seems to be 5 p.m., just when I'm getting stuck into a meeting or list of emails. Meanwhile, I have to duck my head in shame as yet again I do not volunteer to do anything for the school fair, not even the tidying up.

There I am, telling myself that I will have only one To Do List and in fact having eight, spread between an out-of-sorts pink Filofax, a hand-held computer, and various bits of paper. There I am, getting home for bedtime three or four weekday nights (big tick), but in reality coming in, sitting down at the computer

TOP TIP

If you are overloaded with lots of competing obligations, learn to treat your life like crop rotation! In other words, allow yourself to give priority to some things at the expense of others some of the time.

and continuing where I left off at my desk (bad mark). And there I am, saying I'm not working at weekends and in reality often sinking into an exhausted stupor as soon as Saturday comes and being no good to anybody.

Most of us recognize the living-like-an-egg-timer syndrome. Whichever way I spin it to myself, I work for more hours a week than I don't; no matter how much I thin out my diary, it always fattens back up again; no matter how much I plan and organize, I leave something out, like those bits of balloon that pop out when one end is squeezed and squeezed again.

CASE STUDY

Sophie, a writer, is married to Dan, a film-maker.
I started to work from home only about five years ago. I found it really hard, coming home after a busy day in the office, knowing as you put your key in the lock that there are going to be all sorts of other demands made of you. You take a deep breath and then you're in. There will be arguments to test King Solomon, homework to help with that is way beyond your academic capacity, or vital pieces of clothing or sheets of school info to find. It used to amaze me how much responsibility would seem to be mine. In my head I would be wondering how it ever got like this. There was always so much left for me to deal with: running up and down those stairs like a maniac, hoovering while I carried the washing down the stairs.

Not that it was always like that. Sometimes I would come home and there would be smells of supper cooking, and everyone would be doing their homework or music practice, and it would all seem as if everything was fine without me. Then one part of me felt sad while the other wanted to step away, take advantage of it, and go and do something else.

Juggling and Struggling and Muddling Along

In short, I veer between extremes like most working parents, just as I multitask not just because I'm good at it but because I *have* to do it, like it or not. Women and men are driven by all sorts of feelings as we juggle and struggle and muddle along, including fear: that someone else will take our job; that there won't be enough money; that if we don't organize a million things for our children they will be denied some kind of Personal Development holy grail; or that we will 'forget' how to do it. Either way, we generally don't feel we have a choice because often we have only limited choices.

There is Lauren the radio producer who, having dropped her son at his three-hour-per-day nursery, spent most of her second maternity leave 'running' back home to feed the baby with little more than turn-around time before she had to get back to the nursery. There's Habie, the market researcher and writer who, although childless, gets less sleep than a parent with small children because she stays up half the night writing her novels and reports. And there's Steve, the computer software entrepreneur who makes his excuses to dash to an imaginary meeting in order to scoot to school to catch his daughter in her assembly. Steve doesn't want to miss the event but the culture doesn't let him easily or flexibly take the time off – yet.

Even celebrities are beginning to talk in interviews about balance as much as about their latest product. Take Madonna, who told *Elle* magazine that no matter how hard she tries to juggle her family and work commitments, she still suffers from permanent guilt as a mother. Then there has been the pitiful sight of watching Britney

 TOP TIP

Learn your limits and don't push yourself to breaking point. That means doing what it takes to avoid letting exhaustion accumulate until something snaps.

Spears disintegrate and reinvent herself for the profit of all the paparazzi and her record company rather than her children (who she lost custody of in the process). The celebrity work ethic doesn't appear to be very family-friendly and it is debatable whether it creates lasting happy families either.

CASE STUDY

Marie, a masseuse from France, is married to an Englishman. They have two children, a girl aged nine and a boy aged five.

When my daughter was small I got an au pair and took a job as a music publisher. I felt very out of control and unfulfilled in every way. There was no work–life balance – it was tipping this way and that, and so it was more like a See-Saw. I was unhappy about the way the au pair spoke about my daughter when I got home and I really didn't like the way I felt when I was at work. I think I was naive about managing a demanding job in which people raised their eyebrows and looked pissed off if you left at six in the evening while leaving my precious kids with someone who didn't want to look after them.

So I simply stopped. Despite the financial repercussions (and these were considerable) I just couldn't go on like that. My husband found it really difficult because he had always seen me as a high-powered woman, and it took a lot of adjustment for me too. I would be at a music group where these mothers would be singing along to nursery rhymes and I wouldn't even know the song, I was that much out of the loop.

Then I trained in massage and took on a few jobs for money when my second son was in school. The main thing is that now I feel much more in control. I have completely changed my life for the sake of my kids and I am happy about that.

The M-Word

I have mentioned men already but only in passing. That is because this book is not intended to cover them in any depth (which made some of them very cross indeed) and, statistically speaking, it isn't about them. The vast (and I do mean vast) majority of women are responsible for childcare in this country and there is still a vast (and, at more than 17 per cent, I do mean vast) pay gap between the genders. So I admit that when I first started out on the idea for this book, I was clear – as was my male publisher – that this was therefore a book for women.

However, I quickly encountered two reactions from men. One was Hurt: 'Why aren't you asking me what I think?' The other was Hurt's cousin, Outrage: 'How bloody cheeky,' they said. 'You are writing about how hard and tough and difficult it is for women, but what about us? We have to be either the breadwinner so you can give up work and concentrate on being earth mothers, or we have to stay at home and do all the nappy duty because the job market has meant it is easier for women to find better-paid work than us. Or,' voices rising, 'you just don't give us credit for being in the same soup as you, trying to have the soul, the spirit, and the wallet working in glorious harmony.'

Certainly my husband Alaric, who is the house-spouse looking after our children for most of the working week, can't help reflecting that women like me, who wanted it all, now feel every bit of the exhaustion, confusion, and resentment that the once-exclusively male breadwinners felt when women by and large stayed at home.

In partnerships in which men do significant amounts of childcare, the mother and father often experience two apparently contradictory emotions. On the one hand the father can feel as alienated as traditional housewives once did. So Alaric has refused to come to dinner parties with me 'because I have nothing to say; all I have done is the washing and the cleaning'. He says, 'You may not have to do all the tedious stuff

I do, all the washing and cooking and cleaning, but what you do is fulfilling and gets recognition from others'. True enough, but on the other hand I often secretly envy him for not having to go to an office or engage in the politics of work, and for having the house to himself during the day whilst I'm rushing around in traffic trying to make my next meeting and

minding terribly that I feel guilty and overloaded to boot. That's the contradiction that faces all working parents. but it feels particularly tough being a woman and finding that liberation is not completely fine and dandy when we basically thought it could be, should be, and would be.

So, I stand corrected on the men front as far as this book is concerned. Men like my husband wear the pinny while their wives and partners wear the trousers, and while it isn't the norm it is much more the norm than I thought. Sorry, guys.

CASE STUDY

Sam, a stay-at-home dad to children aged five, three, and two, is married to an NHS manager.

We didn't meet until we were in our late thirties, so there was a sense of having to get a move on and make a family. I was a landscape designer with my own business but neither of us wanted someone else to look after our kids. While I can pick up where I left off when the kids are older, the same can't be said for my wife's job.

It has a very distinct career path that doesn't do stops and starts.

Now I moan with the other mothers about Sue not being that interested in my day and we swap stories about being taken for granted, or our partners forgetting to phone and warn us that they are going to be late when we are desperate for an adult conversation. At least women know now that it is not a gender thing when the person who brings home the bacon has to cut off a bit from what is going on at home, and then finds it hard to make the adjustment from an adult work life when plunged straight into the madness and unpredictability of small children.

I don't feel unmanned by being the stay-at-home person. I think I'm much less panicky and more philosophical about it than the mothers I go to the park with. I have to say that quite a few of my male friends who have kids are jealous of me, something they admit only after a few pints.

Having It Some... But Not Having It All

There is something particularly lonely about being all dressed up for work in a playground of non-working mums. You have to endure those looks that mix pity, envy, and outright disapproval. It is a bit like wearing a sign that says, 'Sorry, Bad Mum, no PTA duty for me, I'm too busy,' which these days is a bit like driving a gas-guzzling car around a bunch of cyclists or saying you are a banker: you are going to get evil looks and you know it.

Whilst men are applauded for wanting to climb the career ladder and get home just in time to put the kids to bed, or are admired when they give up work to bring up the children (Alaric's house husbandry is discussed by playground parents in the hushed tones usually reserved for someone famous), those of us who combine work with motherhood enjoy no such status. In this culture we have nightmares that our children will end up on drugs because we *weren't there* or it makes us guilty that we haven't got children because we *put ourselves first*. Finger wagging is all around us, and the fingers being wagged are often our own as much as others'.

This attitude towards the working mum is, I'm sad to say, often voiced by women who have given up work to stay at home and terrorize the school PTA for their day job, whilst secretly panicking that they will either die of boredom or never get back on the job ladder. And it is also voiced by our mothers' generation, those who began to 'Have It All' in the 1960s and who have watched with mounting concern the effect that liberation has had on the lives of their daughters – as well as their sons. And, of course, it has more than a grain of truth to it. We have more power, yes. We can rise up the career ladder, yes. But there is another truth, too: now that it is the norm for both women and men to go out to work, it has become harder to combine making a living with having quality time, including time for making love. And hard truths hurt.

So we know: equality has its price. We are still working for a living and not lolling around rolling in lolly instead. In addition, the explosion in the number of separated parents means that an awful lot of us have to juggle our family time just to stand still – by organizing parental visits to our exes and managing as a single parent. So it isn't that surprising that the prevailing wisdom today is still that if we multitask we must inevitably multi-fail. I have just given plenty of evidence for the prosecution in terms of my own rushed lifestyle.

> ☞ **TOP TIP**
>
> Learn to multi-task meanfully: download newspaper podcasts to listen to while washing up.

Banish Your Inner Monster Mummy

But hang on a minute! I'm not buying this 'We are all bad and have to choose between career fulfilment or family' nonsense. It simplifies something extremely complicated, something that defines modern societies: choice. We have choice and we need to know how to choose, as well as how to improve our choices. Some of this involves government and employers, of course, but an awful lot involves us, individually.

On top of this, you might be making assumptions, such as thinking that I must be failing my children because I work a lot. But am I? I mean, maybe I'm failing them because of other failures on my part that will scar them emotionally for life, but would do so even if I had baked them flapjacks and ironed the creases into their PJs. And then again, maybe I'm not a bad mother anyway. Or at all. Maybe I am a better mother than the one who has 'given up' everything to be at the school gates but is seething with unused capability.

I bet I *do* fail my children. I know that sometimes I don't listen closely to what they tell me. One of their favourite stories is 'When Mum Turned into a Monster'. They particularly like the bit where the exhausted and exasperated mum turns green and gnarly in the supermarket. Sometimes they wish for a different family altogether. Does this sound familiar? It should, because family factions, feuds, and frictions didn't start with Women's Lib. They're just life. And anyway, what works for one kid at one stage in their life is, maddeningly, totally wrong for another. I can – and do – blame myself some of the time, but I might be missing the point by doing so.

This doesn't mean I'm cavalier and think there is no point trying. I try very, *very* hard to do right by everyone, including myself. I just don't want to live by other people's edicts and expectations of the norm. I don't want to spend energy thinking I should be different or better; I just want to feel that I am doing better at getting closer to my ideal – not

TOP TIP

Don't compare your family to other families. Compare it only to your values and what you think is best for it. If you aren't doing what is best for your family or for you, change may be necessary. But avoid Family Envy where you think everyone else is doing it better than you – because I bet they aren't.

yours. And my ideal is shaped – as it must be – by my values, and those of my husband. In other words: what we want, not what we're told we must do.

Tempting though it is, I don't want to cave in to guilt and shame that somehow working very hard means I'm greedy for success. For second-generation feminists born in the 1960s like me, who sported badges saying: 'A woman without a man is like a fish without a bicycle,' it is particularly hard to accept the charge that we have opened Pandora's Box by embracing our careers as warmly as our families. I don't think cycling backwards is particularly good progress, do you?

So I combine work and life at a hectic pace. I realize that sometimes this means that my family have to share me with my work; that my children have to share me with each other; that my attention to work gets interrupted by my home life; that my aged parents see less of me than they should; that my husband often gets my time least and last of all. These are the pitfalls of the See-Saw life, and there is nothing super-heroic about them.

Many circumstances may conspire to make you feel totally at

TOP TIP

Stop being perfectionist, instead aim for being 'Good Enough'.

the mercy of your See-Saw life: you may be single and want to be wedded, or childless and want children, or are caring for someone sick, or are very unwell yourself, or work in a job or a culture you hate. More often than not, the See-Saw might feel permanently weighted to the bottom.

CASE STUDY

Ginny, forty-three, is a speech therapist and has no children.
I am having to face the very real possibility that I might never have children. There is really nothing that anyone can say to make that all right for me. I didn't choose childlessness but I did get hooked up with someone too early. When we broke up I was in my late thirties. Afterwards I found it very hard to meet someone.

My work is very fulfilling, and I have great friends as well as a very active life, but I'm pretty desperate about my situation. My work–life balance is fairly good but, you know what, I don't really want it to be. I really envy my friends with babies, until it has got to the stage where I find it hard to go and visit friends' newborns because I am worried I might cry. In fact I have cried and had to pretend that I was overwhelmed with joy when in fact I was overwhelmed with envy.

When I am feeling very happy, I tell myself that it's fine because I will fill my life up, work for a charity, and be able to do the risky things that mothers wouldn't want to do. On other days I feel pathologically depressed about it. I find myself more and more drawn to my cats but try to resist it because I don't want to become a sad old lady with cat hair down my back and a house that smells of tomcats.

However, no matter how trapped we feel, we aren't, at least not completely. We may be in a vicious circle of work-to-live rather than live-to-work; and we may feel badly out of sync with some aspect of our lives. In fact I'd bet on it. But that doesn't mean we can't rebalance, rearrange what we do and how we do it. Just a bit. Just enough. You can always improve a bland dish with a bit of seasoning, or turn down the heat and opt for slow cooking.

Getting Off the Perfection Treadmill

You aren't going to wake up tomorrow morning to find that you've won the lottery and have a perfect life, but getting off the perfection treadmill is a good place to start figuring out what works for you and those around you. In fact, getting off any kind of treadmill is recommended, because the chances are that you never really chose to get on in the first place.

My main recipe for surviving the downs of the See-Saw – the depression, the guilt, the exhaustion, the uncertainty, the frustration – has been to learn how to take stock of what matters, to constantly experiment with recipes for everything from ways to get the basics done with little time, to relaxing properly. Use books like this, talk to others, get a life coach, get a therapist... Get some help. This isn't an argument for introspection or self-obsession, but it is to say that some of the fog only clears with concentration and help from others or time together thinking it through.

I still love the old joke about the musician who asked a taxi driver for directions to the Albert Hall. The driver looked at the man clutching a violin case and said, 'The same way you get anywhere in life: practice, practice, practice.'

WORKING MUM'S PARENTING TIPS OFTEN BREACH HEALTH AND SAFETY LAWS

2

See-Saw Cissies

Oh, whinge, whinge. Poor me. I work so hard. I never get to see the children! My mortgage is so expensive! I'm so tired all the time! Yawn, yawn. 'Get on with it, woman,' says my Inner Voice. 'You lead a lucky, varied, well-paid life, so enough, already.'

I shall stop talking to myself. Or you can join in. Tell me to shut up and stop complaining. I worry that in having the time to worry about the See-Saw, I can't really have anything to worry about at all. Because I'm a good Jewish girl, worrying and I are best friends. So I begin to worry about something else. Maybe I *don't* have anything to worry about! Maybe my life is perfect: healthy kids; more or less lovely husband; lovely new kitchen extension (OK, now scarily expensive since the credit cruch nearly doubled the mortgage, but it is lovely). Something is bound to go wrong…

And just because I *do* like my life and feel lucky, pretty happy and

TOP TIP

Keep a daily tally of three
manageable things you want to
achieve, not thirty. List them
and do them.

fulfilled doesn't mean that I'm a cissy for wanting someone to say, at least occasionally, 'There, there.' Of course, like many self-respecting, ball-breaking feminists I'm a total cissy some of the time. I'm unable to contain my hysterics if I see those little-things-with-tails-I-can't-mention-or-I'll-scream as they saunter across our floor, looking for all the world as if they pay the mortgage, not me. While it's true that I once dissolved into tears when my car broke down (I *refuse* to know what's under the bonnet on top of everything else), do not, however, mess with me in the boardroom, or try to queue-jump me in the petrol station on the Holloway Road. Then I'm not a cissy at all.

Was I the only one convinced I was living on a See-Saw? Clearly I needed to ask others whether they felt the same. I needed a focus group, so I began to accost everyone I knew. This earned me stiff rebukes from my children. 'Stop talkin' to them, Mummy, talk to me!' instructed my youngest, Wolfie, who is nearly four, as I tried to inter-rogate my friend Caitlin while walking him to nursery. It is hard enough to walk children to school at the best of times. (I wish I could say what hell it is getting three children ready and out of the door in an hour but it's actually I who take the most time to get ready, with all that middle-aged make-up routine.)

The primary schoolers were even less accommodating. 'Mum, why are you sooooo embarrassing?' said Roman, who is ten. 'Walk on the other side of the road and pretend you don't know me,' he commanded as I announced I wanted to straw poll the parents about how busy they felt. Exactly what passes muster as a cool mum activity is something that continues to elude me. He may have a point but I stood my ground.

Singing Like Canaries

As conversation-openers go, saying, 'I'm writing about work–
life balance and how none of us
knows what it means except that
we all feel obsessed by it,' could

TOP TIP

Take comfort in the knowledge
that you are not alone in your
struggle to muddle and juggle
along: there is reassurance, if
not safety, in numbers.

have produced a big yawn. Initially I worked on little more than a
hunch that, while the whole question of life's See-Saw wasn't just my
bugbear, it also wasn't the number one topic of conversation. In the
summer of 2008 when I started to write this book, the talk at the
water cooler was more about the credit crunch. I suppose what I
didn't know was whether the subject was one that bored people, or
didn't affect them, or whether they felt 'talked out' about it, in the
way I feel talked out about post-baby sagginess, or keeping the
marital magic going, or – excuse me while I stifle an irritated groan –
the Which School? Debate and the invariable bust-up about state
versus private.

Luckily, once I had run the gauntlet of my kids' mortification
about my straw poll, everyone wanted to talk. In fact, they wanted to
share in a big way. Far from getting an uninterested reaction to my
casual vox pop on the subject, as a rule a funny kind of 'Yes, you
asked me about my secret obsession' look would come into their

eyes, and they would crane
forward almost needily before
invariably launching into their
take on the subject. To say that
people began to sing like canaries
about their experiences is an
understatement.

TOP TIP

Be flexible in your approach
because circumstances can
change, either with you or with
your children. Review your set-
up at least every six months to
assess what is working well
and what isn't.

Habie, forty-four, a freelance market researcher and writer, lives in London. Single with no children, she is aunt to six nephews and nieces – her 'niblings'.

To me, having work–life balance is not cissy at all. It means being disciplined enough to say *no* to a client sometimes. It means making my own life a priority after another endless spell of work that has left no time to see even my beloved niblings up the road, let alone have a haircut, do volunteer work with asylum seekers and other activities that actually matter to me more than my work, print my photos from India or see friends and family long neglected. It means making time for life by making a conscious decision to say *no* to work and *yes* to life, regularly.

In a more general sense, it means not letting the stresses of work invade non-work times to the point where it ruins them. You might be walking in the park with a loved one, but can only think about why your client was rude to you or how you will get a report written. You don't even notice the golden evening sunlight and, worse still, you alienate the person you're with by being a coiled spring of anxiety, because work has taken over your soul, instead of just your time.

Most of all, work–life balance means being well organized. There is often *no excuse* for cancelling your personal life in favour of work, or having days when you give time to neither because you're stressing about both. Don't imagine that it is a trivial issue to get it wrong: this stuff is deadly serious for our lives.

One evening after work I collected my daughter Anoushka who is eight from a play date. I arrived to find Phil, her friend's father, cooking supper while the girls jumped about in the garden on a trampoline, squealing with joy. When I told Phil I was writing this book he looked positively animated. 'Men like me are trying to help the women in our lives get better work–life balance by doing things like this,' he said, pointing to the table laid for supper and

TOP TIP

Divide your To Do List in a way that brings focus and allows you to tick things off. This could be separating 'doing' from 'sorting', or 'children' from 'work', or 'now' from 'tomorrow'. Create a system that works and that you will want to keep, rather than just for its own sake.

returning to stir the food he was cooking. His wife Anne was still at the office. They run an architectural practice but it suits both of them for Phil to do the after-school childcare some of the time. Anne and I usually play telephone ping-pong for a couple of weeks before managing to actually finalize a play date for our daughters and we often discuss our lack of time and commiserate with each other about it. For those of us who employ ourselves it can be both easier and harder. Easier because you can choose your juggling without asking permission; harder because the buck stops with you for work, making it harder to say 'stop' at any given point when you could always, always do a bit more.

Stories from the Juggling Front Line

As I continued to consider the seeming impossibility of work–life balance, examples of See-Saw living began to leap out at me constantly. Talking to a friend about petrol prices elicited the surprise confession that she spends quite a lot of time sitting in her stationary car, going nowhere, not to save money, but to listen to *The Archers* just before she officially 'gets home' from work. 'It's my only me-time,' she explains.

TOP TIP

Don't plan and diarize everything. Learn to be spontaneous – about anything from play dates to seeing family or friends. Sometimes it is quicker and puts an end to doing everything in work mode all the time.

An old friend came to visit who now lives in Africa and works for the UN. We spent most of the time talking, not about the politics of Africa but with great intensity about how she managed to travel regularly to UN headquarters in New York leaving behind a small child. The conclusion: it's easier to be two years old than to split yourself in two. Whether you leave one country to 'go to work' or another to come home to your house, the issues are the same: my friend's See-Saw regularly swings downward in parenting terms and upward in career terms... until she gets off the plane back home and lands on her own floor with the toys once more.

I know men who are worn out from trying to be the breadwinner and the perfect dad, just as I know women in the same position. We'd all like to win a lottery that pays out time, because our lives eat up the very thing we value most, minutes, hours, days and years.

CASE STUDY

Alan, forty-nine, is a marketing director with two sons aged ten and nine. He was divorced two years ago.

I'm afraid with me it was that classic thing of having no work–life balance at all. I was working very long hours and missing out on all those important events – sports days, school plays, even parents' evenings. If it was a See-Saw, it was very much weighted down on one side by work.

22

When my wife left me it was a wake-up call. I couldn't be one of those dads who lose touch with th when they divorce. My ex-wife agreed to them staying with Wednesday and every other weekend. In a way I got to know n ons again in a much purer way because I didn't have my wife acting as a buffer or imposing the way she thought I should be with them. I think we have a really good, relaxed relationship. On the Wednesdays and Fridays that they are here, I leave work early to pick them up. My employers were pretty surprised by this because they knew what I was like when the kids were young but they can't really complain because I come in early on those days.

It is pretty tragic that it took my wife leaving for me to realize that I had no work–life balance whatsoever.

I certainly don't know anyone, even couples with good incomes and good support systems, who finds combining work and daily life anything other than a major assault course for much of the time. My escapist summer reading

TOP TIP

Switch off for as little as five minutes every day and don't do anything with your mind or hands or time.

last year wasn't romantic fiction; it was a business book about how to reduce your time to a four-hour working week. Isn't that the fantasy we all have now?

Obviously there is no single answer, no ideal of perfection; only questions and choices – and all too limited ones at that.

Shyama, divorced, works from home and has two daughters.

I do think there is an element of spoiled-little-girl whinging when the issue of work–life balance is raised. When I hear women in designer clothes who enjoy an expense-account lifestyle complaining that life isn't fair, it turns my stomach.

In my circle, most complaints rest on the nature of the woman's home relationship. It's not about work versus home, it's about the abrogation of responsibility within that home by the male partner. Women shoulder an unfair load, which makes them short-tempered with their children and constantly tired. This leads to guilt, under-scored by resentment.

The easiest way to deal with the problem is to throw money at it – by eating out, going abroad on holiday, employing entertainers for birthday parties where the whole class is invited. But instead of lessening the stress, this increases it, and so the cycle continues.

Catch-22

The BBC once sent a taxi to collect me for an interview late one night. I made conversation with the driver who told me about himself. He was a doctor who had escaped from the Taliban in Afghanistan just before he qualified. Under UK law he would have had to spend a further five years retraining to catch up with his original qualifications. So he became a taxi driver. He had a wife and young child but had to work seven days to cover his living costs and tax. He had a life, but no time to live it.

This wasn't the See-Saw as a jolly juggle, all balls in the air and smug self-congratulation. This was about not having any work–life balance to speak of. I wouldn't normally compare myself to an Afghani taxi driver, except that I found myself thinking how alike we all are in feeling that we work to live rather than live to work, even those of us who are not night drivers.

CASE STUDY

Jonathan, forty, a media lawyer with three daughters under twelve, lives in St Albans.

When we first met, my wife was earning more than me as an executive in an advertising company. She stopped working after our first daughter was born and there has never been any question of her working, even though the youngest is now coming up to six.

There is a big part of me that is really envious of my wife because I would love to see the girls more and find it very hard to go back to work after the holidays. When I ring her up from the office and she has just come back from an exercise class or meeting her friends for lunch, I feel quite resentful. I know that bringing up kids is really hard work but I would love to work less and for us to share being with the kids more.

It's the most difficult subject for us because my wife says that she's unemployable now and thinks things are fine as they are. The trouble is that my job is not the most secure in the world and I really can't talk to her about it because we are in such different worlds. I feel I have been pushed into being a provider who doesn't see his kids and I am really not happy about it.

Whatever your See-Saw, I have two pieces of advice to stop you feeling like a cissy.

First: don't compare yourself to others. Worry is relative. Your problems may be tiny or they may be huge, and you might be the kind of person who makes mountains out of molehills or the kind who endures all sorts of nightmares with grace and elegance.

The second is: don't, absolutely don't, listen to the 'pull yourself together' types if you are feeling overwhelmed. Only you know whether you have a lot to be grateful for or need to have a big boohoo. Sometimes it's helpful to have a major panic and a meltdown to really get your problems in perspective and work out what might bring some relief. But I'll admit I don't get much sympathy when I stand on a chair yelling about those-little-things-with-tails-I-can't-mention. Any tips on that front are most welcome.

On the See-Saw: Shirley

Shirley is a single mother of two young daughters. She is the founder of Silverhawk, a recruitment business specializing in flexible work for working parents.

At the risk of being controversial, I don't buy into the terminology 'work–life balance'. It assumes that something is always about to become out of kilter and that life is an inevitable struggle. I try to adopt a more integrated approach. It helps me to live by the concept of 'Enough Already', which means:

- Enough *focus to make you excellent at your chosen profession (without having to rely on your job for your self-esteem).*
- Enough *emotional energy to provide the nurturing care that a child, parent, partner or friend needs (without hovering over every aspect of their lives).*
- Enough *effort to create a beautiful home, open to friends and family (whilst still ensuring that it is your sanctuary).*
- Enough *dates in the diary to provide culture, entertainment, and sharing with friends – food for the soul (without having to see and be seen at three events in one evening).*
- Enough *air miles to travel and experience life's differences (without having to stay in five-star hotels and sit only at the front of the plane).*
- Enough *self-control not to answer unnecessary calls or emails on the BlackBerry (without ignoring those that will help others to make key decisions or make them feel you care).*
- Enough *exercise to keep fit (without having to run a marathon).*
- Enough *good food and rest to keep healthy (without denying yourself alcohol and carbs after 6 p.m.).*
- Enough *confidence to say no – it's enough already!*

RECIPE

RECIPE: SHREDDED LISTS

TIME: Ten minutes to half an hour.

INGREDIENTS: A system of organizing your 'To Dos', including a filing system and a shredding machine.

If you love lists, you will love this recipe. But even if you don't, you will love the feeling of achievement and control that this recipe brings. Take all those school notes, bank statements, medical notes, receipts, catalogue-torn sheets with the shoes you like or the special offer or indeed anything in paper which needs... sorting. Create a sorting system which pleases you. I'm a bit of a Stationery Queen, so I love endlessly creating new in-trays. But the point is simple: be able to find anything you might look for or need, in under a minute. How you label, sort, organize is your business, but I do recommend a fabulous book called *Getting Things Done* by David Allen if you need tips.

The shredder is a good idea because on a weekly basis you need to watch yourself pleasingly shred that To Do List you DID or get rid of the aforementioned records and reminders that don't need a permanent home: in which case take them out of 'To Do' and put them somewhere labelled clearly... Think of this as the jam-making See-Saw recipe, with neatly labelled jars full of juicy stuff you have managed to make nice and tasty instead of leaving a sour taste in the 'I'll get round to it but I'm too disorganized right now' mouth. My lips are puckering in sympathy right now.

3

The Thirty-Six-Hour Day

Some people want peace of mind. Or early retirement. Or better health. Or, to be trivial, an unlimited supply of new season Emma Hope shoes. Oh, and a glamorous Mulberry bag. Whatever we really, really want, we definitely want more hours in the day, plain and simple. As the world has moved from 24/7 to 24/nanosecond, with something happening all the time – but less time to actually spend because of work pressures and the general culture – the only thing that most of us long for, more than more sleep, is more daytime hours in which to get everything done.

The Time Monster

The schedule, the diary, and the To Do Lists have become staples of the basic way that those of us who work manage our time, with or without children. I schedule everything from 7 a.m. onwards, and then find that time, like fingers on a hand, runs out mid-count. It's not as if a time monster is stealing my hours, it just feels like it. Certainly it is easy to think someone or something is doing all this time-stealing to poor little me, when in fact I'm the one who is trigger-happy on the old computer or phone keyboard and no one else.

CASE STUDY

Linda, a social worker, is single with four children aged from eight to sixteen.

I decided to go back and study after the children's father left us. I was determined that the kids wouldn't miss out and that I would get a good degree and a decently paid job so that they could have the experiences and things that other kids had.

When my youngest was only three I managed to get him a nursery place and then had to rely on after-school clubs and holiday schemes. Sometimes my mother helped out, but not on a regular basis. I really lived day to day and mostly got away with it (except when the children became ill or hurt themselves at school). I managed to get them to school, go to college, pick them up from after-school club, and then get back home to deal with supper, homework, and their activities.

I also made a real decision that they would be able to do all the extra-curricular stuff I could possibly manage. They have each done loads of things – gymnastics, football, violin lessons, swimming – which did involve a lot of travelling around so that they could go to matches and competitions. Of course I didn't always feel like spending my weekends driving across London but I always did it.

Part of the problem is that there is no longer an 'off' switch, now that mobiles bleep texts and emails can be read all the time, anywhere. I recently sat next to a woman on the tube who was texting furiously. Text after text, head bent. I wondered whether she had some kind of amazing mobile network that worked underground. 'Oh no, they are just being stored, but I like doing them here,' was her reply. If this was something else she was doing pointlessly, it would be called obsessive-compulsive disorder. Not for nothing are we workies in danger of being labelled 'CrackBerries'.

Information is coming at us and we respond to those winking in-boxes immediately. Did we instantly reply to every letter in the olden days? What did we do before mobiles, before email? I think we waited. I think we achieved as much, but differently. When I was young and worked in the press office at Penguin Books in the early 1980s, I had to call the novelist Edna O'Brien, who had a new fangled thing – an answerphone. The message stated that before the beep there would be a pause, and then she said something wonderfully writerly in her slow Irish lilt: 'It will give you time to think.' I still remember everything about hearing that message, twenty-five years ago. They felt like the wisest words that I should keep in mind for decades to come. Yes, Thinking Time!

CASE STUDY

Ray, thirty-five, is head of communications in a global firm and has one stepdaughter.

I am as interested in the whole work–life balance thing as anyone else. Clearly this question affects men as well as women. For me the big issue is boundaries. Where does work end and life begin?

For example, if I spend an enjoyable evening at a dinner with some key figures from the political, business, and media worlds, I can't easily pigeon-hole that into the strictly 'work' box; it's more like a middle path of 'network'. That said, I limit myself to a maximum of four out of seven nights out.

The biggest curse to switching off is the epitome of being switched on, literally: the joint telephone and emailer device. It is terribly easy to get sucked into looking at emails and then responding, simply by switching on the phone to make a call!

The key for me to balancing on the See-Saw is being very rigorous about boundaries. Come what may, I'm in the gym every weekday morning at 6.30 a.m. and, come what may – although this may sound a bit metrosexual – I finish the working week on a Friday with a Pilates class at 6.30 p.m. to formally close the week.

Of course in jobs like mine there are unscheduled events and times when the phone rings or I need to work, but I like to make a distinction between problems that can be solved in the week and a true crisis, which is generally rare and for which you drop everything, obviously.

Multiple Diary Hell

Before I can think, I have to know what is on the schedule, because without it I'm lost in a hopeless tangle of confusion. Things pile up and I'm on six back-to-back meetings a day, one of which takes place... on the other side of town.

Part of the problem with schedules – be they on BlackBerries, organized by assistants, or just in our heads, running unconsciously on automatic pilot – is that you get dependent on them and then they become like a bad sat-nav: you end up in the wrong place at the wrong time. And anyway, not to sound too completely Eeyore-like, schedules are exactly like the weather: just when it is all sunny and easy peasy, something comes along to change everything and you have to begin again (as well as

TOP TIP

Take an aerial view of your life. Do you really need to squeeze a play date in after school for each child? Or seven meetings a day? Take a step back and look at what you can take *out* of the diary rather than what you can squeeze in.

match all the *versions* of your paper-plus-electronic schedule to boot).

The problems start when trying to schedule a meeting in which more than two people need to be at. In house-buying they call it the chain. With work–life balance it is Multiple Diary Hell. For my father's ninety-first birthday my family planned to celebrate with a meal at his favourite local Indian restaurant. My parents, my two brothers and I all live within a couple of miles of one another. But it took a good week of phone calls and emails, plus a last-minute *reschedule*, to finally get us together. I almost wish there had been no consultation, no back-and-forth: just a deadline and a 'Be there or be square'.

Likewise, any scheduling delay can cause a time pile-up. My children's school sends through the timetable for parents' evening, asking us to choose a time slot (which we may or may not get; it's a get-there-first lottery) and then I have to block the diary potentially ('pencil it in') until I know whether I will have that slot. If not, it takes the same amount of time again to re-ravel what has just unravelled.

Instant Gratification

I learned that rather than tie myself up in diary knots it was quite useful, sometimes, to be spontaneous. I began to see how it was possible to leave some space between meetings, then call or email a person I needed or wanted to see, and say, 'I'm going to be in town this afternoon, I don't suppose you are free for a coffee?' This cut out the middle man of the iCal or Outlook or the plain old diary.

At first it feels very odd, almost weird, as if I'm *failing* by having any free time at all! But thanks to mobile technology and fabulous cafes and clubs, it is very rare to find yourself unable to do any work of any kind, anywhere. So, when inevitably your spontaneous efforts don't pay off, your time is not that worst of all things (shudder): wasted. In any case, I would say that two thirds of the time I do my 'Now' thing, it actually works. (Not with dentists, obviously. And not with head teachers. And not with all sorts of people… But come on, imagine what I'm getting at.)

I began to appreciate the benefit of unscheduled time when I realized how lovely it was to have ten or fifteen minutes to myself when a lunch guest was delayed. They would arrive huffing and puffing with stress, while I felt serene, having briefly tuned out and watched the world around me. Quite apart from anything else, it is like visual gossip: you do pick up on other rather intriguing meetings. Just taking in the surrounding bustle is a very good way to unwind.

Since I have taken up walking around Central London between meetings as a form of exercise I have also realized how liberating it feels to spend ten minutes or so diverting through a park or finding time for a quick coffee somewhere delicious like Soho's Bar Italia. And a spontaneous stroll through Russell Square Gardens en route to Holborn or through St James' Park en route to Westminster is a great kind of refreshment. More and more cities have regenerated parks: find one if you possibly can.

Time-Stretching

If spontaneity sounds like time-wasting, then try this: Time-Stretching. Of course, most of us know that this modern rushing about is madness at some level, but no amount of books about taking it slowly or of opting out of the weary rat race really help those of us who have to do a lot. It's important to just recap why we *must*, since I think many of us feel particularly targeted by a trendy view that to run around doing too much is self-indulgent and selfish. Well, that's as may be, but it is often also to raise incomes and families, to keep our brains moving, or to keep from failing in our duties to others. Some of the work–life balance tips that I now know work for me were born of desperation: if I couldn't have thirty-six hours in every day, how could I make each hour stretch a bit further?

Before I can tell you how I managed Time-Stretching, the business part of me has to introduce you to another S-word, to make sense of what can otherwise be a life of diary hell: Strategy. We need to review the decisions we make about the things we agree or plan to do. This means taking enough of a breather to look hard at these decisions, bearing in mind that there are only a maximum of twelve to fifteen workable hours in a day, and sort out what needs to give. This breather is 'Focus Time'.

Focus Time

When our youngest child was still a tiny tot who wouldn't sleep through the night and my new business wasn't itself out of nappies,

TOP TIP

Save your adrenalin and urgency for a crisis, and learn to manage problems calmly. Try and anticipate more and be less the victim of events.

I realized I simply could not get everything done on a daily basis.

Well, you might say, what's new? Trust me, this was different. I felt under intense pressure and began to buckle. As a result, I stretched time the wrong way: instead of giving focus to one or two tasks, I would drown in a whole series of them that had no beginning, middle, or end. When I came home I would twitch with tension and act as if I were doing the children a favour by reading them a story. Actually listening to them, possibly the thing a child wants more than anything, was beyond me. When I did go to bed I felt I had accomplished little apart from another notch on my martyr belt. Marital Quality Time – not the full-on, saucy-snuggly version, just the 'Hello, honey, how was your day' version – was also out of the question.

Suddenly having two primary schoolers in two different playgrounds in the same school felt like a logistical nightmare. Our toddler was waking up in the night for more milk and then wriggling and piggling in bed with us. What can be a delicious bit of baby bonding was just pure sleep deprivation and made me wake up demented with tiredness and stress. During this time my beloved business seemed to have turned into another mouth to feed, sucking me further and further into its never-ending To Do List of demands. I wasn't reaching rock bottom or anything – I have never stopped enjoying my work – but I noticed that my tendency to race towards anything with the word 'biscuit' on the packet was increasing in direct proportion to both my hip width and my stress levels of trying to do it all. I knew I was overreaching myself and decided to figure out what to do to feel back on track.

Of course, realizing you have a problem is the first step to solving it. The second is getting what I like to call Assisted Self-Help, in this case, an absolutely terrific transatlantic life coach called Ginger Cockerham, who specializes in coaching business women

TOP TIP

Try and ration email and texting and see how much time you save.

who want to balance their work and their family lives better.

'Coach Ginger' and I began a series of weekly telephone calls (heaven for a time-obsessed control freak, not to have to make another actual appointment and travel to it) in which she taught me my first big secret about See-Saw living: *it's about giving things up*. For me it was giving up the ideal that I could manage on too little sleep, too much adrenalin, and not enough planning, or what Coach Ginger aptly called 'Focus Time'. This basically means looking afresh at everything you have committed to doing and asking whether you really have to do it, or whether you can let something go.

CASE STUDY

Deborah, a full-time specialist nurse, is a single mother with one ten-year-old daughter and lives in Nottingham.

I think about the See-Saw all the time as I'm always balancing everything. I used to live in London and worked at a hospital doing a job I absolutely loved, but when I became pregnant with my daughter, the father didn't want a baby and we separated. He sees Chloe periodically.

As I had no childcare, I left Chloe in Nottingham with my parents, commuting back at weekends. By the time she was three she was calling her grandmother 'Mummy' and me 'Mum'. Even though I had reduced my days to four, I was missing out as her personality developed and it just wasn't right because I wanted to be the centre of her world. Anyway, I was exhausted with the commute so something had to give. And that something was my cherished career.

I loved my job as a specialist rheumatology HIV nurse and I had to give it up. I had to come back to an area I hadn't lived in for seventeen years, where the culture is weighted towards marriage, even unhappy ones, but not single mothers. I had to get a job in a hospital where my career satisfaction has gone right down. Nothing can replace that old job for me: in the team I worked with, we were like a family. But I have my priorities right: my daughter comes first, followed by work, with as much time as I can find for everything else. I don't have a recipe for success, but I am coping and I can't complain.

A number of my women friends tell me that their big liberation has been giving up cleaning. I wish I could do that but, as I am probably the most non-cleany person I know, it's a bit of a cheat to say that I gave up something I never really started in the first place. However, cleaning and tidiness have a symbolism for women in particular, because they mean we are 'house-proud'. And if we are house-proud, then somehow we are being 'good'. And 'good', of course, is better than 'bad'. So giving things up in order to Stretch Time is brave as well as sensible.

☞ TOP TIP

Choose to let go of something you feel you ought to do but can do without, whether it is cleaning, or networking parties, or visiting friends. Take the time too to think about your real needs and what truly matters to you. Hang on to those things but let go of everything else.

Shyama , writer and teacher, divorced, works from home and has two daughters.

I'm an anal retentive when it comes to the house, particularly because I work from home. I like floors and surfaces gleaming, cushions plumped and symmetrical, toilets smelling of pine. I used to kill myself dashing around after the girls went to school, making beds, putting on washes, getting the place back into order. I'd get angry over the stray shoes and crumpled clothes I'd find in corners: I'd literally be muttering to myself about their untidiness and how they took me for granted.

When I pulled a muscle in my back and couldn't meet my own exacting standards for a few days, amazingly I discovered that life still went on pretty much as before. The lesson is learned. We're far more relaxed now and I have an extra hour every morning for drinking coffee and catching up with the papers and the post.

Higher, Faster, Further

Another Ginger-ism is 'Do your Highest and Best', which means that everyone should do only what they do best for their organization – be that family, department or project. It's a homily akin to 'Don't Sweat the Small Stuff' but with more emphasis on achievement.

Put simply, the 'Highest and Best' idea made me realize that whilst I am awful at certain things, rather than beat myself up about it, I now recognize that generally it means I'm better at other stuff too: we all are. So at work, the IT people, the designers, and the editors were very happy when I stopped trying to do their jobs as well as my own. But by giving attention to other aspects of the business instead, everyone benefitted. And at home, instead of coming home and winding everyone up by being bossy and trying to organize them just as I do at the office (prompting Roman to yell in exasperation, 'You're not the boss of me, you know!'), I would do what for kids is Highest and Best – just being there for them, listening, playing, intervening in squabbles, cuddling.

I used to feel stressed by all the micromanaging I was doing. It is exhausting sitting on someone's shoulders basically nagging rather than letting them know *what* you want to achieve but allowing them space to work out *how* they achieve it. Of course, I sometimes have spectacular relapses, but I now refer to my control freak years in the past tense, which is progress!

Boundary Walls

There is a wonderful book about setting boundaries with children, entitled *Saying No*, by the psychotherapist Asha Phillips. She believes that if parents were less frightened of denying children something because they feel such guilt for not being there enough, they would realize that they are doing their kids a favour. We need to teach our children that hearing 'no' is not the end of the world. At first they may be disappointed, furious, upset, and go into meltdown, but they will emerge stronger than if we just give in each and every time.

I think the same is true of adults. We assume that taking on heavy loads is good. There is a sort of macho power game in office culture about who stays the latest, or who always goes out for a drink or networking, or who takes on yet another committee or commitment. But when we do this, we are often being our own worst enemy rather than a friend to ourselves. Instead of learning how to make time stretch for us, we stretch ourselves into needing, actually *needing*, more hours in the day than we have. We need to tell ourselves 'no'.

TOP TIP

If you feel guilty that you are failing someone you are close to, try and step back and be clear: is it generalized guilt or do you actually need to put something right? Make it a practical issue, not a fully laden emotional drama. Guilt weighs us all down.

Doing... Nothing

The adrenalin of rushing around, being busy, is not the same as having energy. In fact, weirdly, it often masks exhaustion. Weekends can often be worse when all the chores rush out at you, and if you are a parent it is very hard not to succumb to the culture of extra-curricular this or that. Again, if you are a parent, it is very hard to do the thing you perhaps need to do most: sleep.

I heard a wonderful story about someone who apparently recharges their batteries on a monthly basis like this: they check into a hotel, alone. They order room service, have a good meal with a good bottle of wine, and go to sleep early. The next morning they make themselves stay asleep each time they begin to surface, so that by the time they leave the hotel room – not having had sex, or watched telly, or done any sight-

TOP TIP

Be firm when someone tries to overload you with work. It works wonders for your self-esteem and magically you are treated with more respect.

seeing, or anything else you should perhaps do in or from a hotel room for twenty-four hours – they have had a perfect modern holiday: rest.

The other easier and less dramatic way of recharging is to do nothing at home. This means not over-planning activities or even knowing what you are going to do; just allow yourself to be spontaneous, to loll around. My kids love having pyjama days during weekends and holidays, particularly at the start of big breaks like Christmas when their heads are overloaded from learning sums and social lessons alike. They veg out, often with telly but also with books, or drawing, but the only

 TOP TIP

Get enough sleep. Work out how many hours sleep you need and try to reach that average over three or four days. In other words it's fine to be up until midnight or one in the morning if you then get tucked up early to make up for it. The alternative is to feel like a zombie – not a good feeling.

thing they have to do is...
nothing. Of course, they still need
taking out, or running around in
the fresh air, all of that. But they
also need physical and mental
rest, too.

TOP TIP

Accept that some days will be
unproductive and 'fudgey' but
don't beat yourself up about it.

Has this taught you to seek out the thirty-six-hour day? Or to
banish it from your fantasies? Well, until they invent a time-travel
button like live action TV freezing and, really stretch time, I hope
banishing wins the day. Saying 'no' to things and occasionally doing
nothing is good – until there actually are more hours in the day.

4

Little Angels and Devils

Not every woman reading this book is a parent. If you aren't, then, in the immortal words of the TV sports announcer about to put the league tables up on screen, 'Look away now.' For the rest of you, let's get started on our little angels and devils, whom no amount of work can stop being at the centre of our lives.

Slob Mum, Top Mum... and Pushy Mum

You know that nursery rhyme about the little girl who had a little curl, right in the middle of her forehead? (And when she was good she was very, very good, but when she was bad, she was horrid.) Well, I may not be horrid, but I'm often terribly bad at balancing when it comes to my children. I don't know a parent who doesn't constantly strive to be better.

Sometimes, I am the epitome of Slob Mum, who can barely summon the energy for bedtime reading. I come home so exhausted after five or six meetings a day, many of them in full adrenalin presentation mode, that I'm next to useless as a companion or mother, and am too tired even to switch off, so I just twitch in front of the telly.

CASE STUDY

Jenny, thirty-four, is a primary school teacher, with two children aged three and six. She has been married for six years to another teacher and they live in Suffolk.

We have swimming, trampolining, and pony-clubbing every evening. It's more important for the children to have some mucking about and hanging around time at home. That's when all the good stuff happens, not when you are bundling them into a car when they are tired and grumpy.

I don't know about everyone else because no one really talks about it, but our house is musical beds nearly every night. We all go to bed in our own beds, but who are we kidding? The kids will get up and try to get into bed with us, or I will leave our double bed because of Rob's snoring and sleep on the sofa, or he will give up because of the kids and go off to sleep in one of their now-empty beds. It would be funny if I wasn't so knackered.

In slob-mum mode I repress the importance of a whole host of routines because it takes too much co-ordination and organization (I draw the line at charts of any kind at home). I wish I could say I'm exaggerating, but ask my husband. Or ask the kids, who often remind me to do their teeth, not vice versa. Euch, I know, but I can't remember everything.

However, in direct contrast, I am also very much Top Mum, too. I know, the amazing two-sided woman: Slob Mum on the one hand and Top Mum on the other! (And if *ET* is on the telly

TOP TIP

Don't be competitive about your children, and especially avoid the Pushy Mum syndrome.

then, obviously, I'm Weepy Mum as well.) When I'm on form, well slept, on the case, and in control, I do manage to be organized and energetic about the children's social lives (so there are play dates galore, holidays booked months ahead, and a varied social life). However, I am less good about organizing extra-curricular lessons, but then I'm fairly anti Pushy Mum syndrome.

And even though I'm definitely Messy Mum, as in not Tidy Mum I do sometimes yank out the paints and stick sheets of paper all over the table, and we do sometimes dance around the same table to loud pop music while Alaric makes Saturday morning waffles and complains that I have interrupted the *Today* programme. I certainly don't feel like a failure when I hear one of my little angels and devils hum to themselves or laugh with each other in a moment of sibling adoration rather than sibling rivalry. In those moments I feel Lovely Mum. And, to boot, Loved Mum.

Not Waving, But Drowning

Getting from working gal to mother was a big transition. In 1997, as the country prepared to shift away from a Conservative Government after a generation to Labour, I prepared a seismic shift of my own: saying adieu to my self-obsessed single life and gaining instant step-motherhood when I got together with Alaric who already had two young children.

47

Rachael was seven and Max was four. I was thirty-two, and Alaric was forty-three. The arrival of these two energetic little primary school kids in my office-girl life was a lovely introduction to the world of children. Up until this point I was doing a reason-ably good impersonation of a character from the PR satire *Absolutely Fabulous*. I was running a PR agency in London's Soho at the time, dashing about organizing press conferences. I really did drink champagne all the time, either in my office or in the newly opened Soho House or the Groucho Club. I worked... and worked... and worked. I would come home to my pretty rooftop flat in Crouch End and conk out. The idea of having a life other than work was beginning to glimmer as a possibility, but I had no idea how to achieve it.

When I first got together with Alaric I was dashing about between London and New York on a monthly basis. He arrived one morning when I was just back. He was highly amused to note that I had rushed away to the Big Apple without entirely clearing up from a dinner party a week earlier. The table was still not completely devoid of empty bottles and cheese plates. I really was Bachelor Girl. Long before I was Slob Mum, I was Slob Single.

Suddenly, thanks to my new boyfriend's children, I was spending weekends getting enthusiastic about sticky birthday cakes, and trips to the zoo and Power Rangers. The first noise I heard in the morning wasn't the whistle of the kettle but the peals of laughter from a curly-haired naughty four year old watching *Teletubbies*. The first present I ever gave Rachael was a copy of *Harry Potter and the Philosopher's Stone* when the cult of Harry wasn't more than a mild publishing success story, not a global phenomenon. How time flies.

Our eldest son Roman was born in 1998. Despite spending every second of the nine months

leading to his birth thinking about it, I felt comprehensively underprepared when the time came. Even though his birth was relatively straightforward, it didn't feel like it to me. I was not waving, but drowning. To say I was frightened is an understatement. My Birth Plan, which I had imagined I would personally run like a clipboard queen presiding over a board meeting, was discarded as real life and real birth took over.

It was a bumpy introduction to parenthood, nothing like as smooth as becoming a step-parent, which actually felt instantly easy. Although I bonded instantly with my tiny son, it would take months for me to feel like I wasn't a bad imposter in someone else's life who was much better than me at all the domestic mothering. I could do the feeding and the cuddling and the showing off the

baby bit, but living life as a mother felt an awful lot harder than going to the office and running a PR campaign. And that realisation was more painful than giving birth.

Polly, forty-four, is a service manager for a charity, with three teenage children. She has been with her Italian partner, Marco, for twenty-one years.

I am not the kind of parent who finds it easy to hand over my kids to someone else, apart from Marco. I tried to graduate how much I worked in careful stages, starting with a part-time respite job that I went off to when Marco came home from work. I slowly built up the number of hours I worked as the kids got older but at one stage I found myself working full time and I nearly cracked up with the strain of it. I was using a childminder, a shared nanny, and friends to fill in. The children were just too young and I couldn't stand that I was missing out on them. My work wasn't worth feeling so bereft because I wasn't with them.

So I deliberately stopped working for a whole term, settled my youngest son into primary school, and have now started the slow build-up of work again.

For both me and Marco, family is the absolute priority: neither of us is particularly ambitious. Family life with all its complications and ups and downs has been wonderful for both of us. He always comes home from work around 4.30 pm even now the children are older, while I come home an hour or so later. He is completely reliable and has never seemed resentful. I don't know if this is because he is Italian and that is what he had when he was young.

Of course, practice makes perfect. By the time our daughter Anoushka was born nearly three years later I was distinctly less anxious and she flamboyantly arrived on 01.01.01 while London celebrated the new year. And by the time our third and youngest child Wolfie was born in

2005, I was so relaxed I had to force myself to stop watching the DVD of *The West Wing* to get to hospital in time.

 TOP TIP

Spend quality time with each child individually in a regular slot each week. Plan to spend more time with them as they progress through childhood, not less.

And now, ten years after my first child was born, I'm finally able to say I think I get the hang of this life of alternating between one mode and another, of going to work in a suit and coming home to hear about playground antics or the importance of a particular toy over another, of watching and listening to my children rather than just ordering them about or imposing routines on them which may not make sense. In short, it can take time to enjoy them while you get out of the haze of simply having them and doing basic care.

Fudge Brain

Regardless of whether you prepared for birth or not, or whether you have an easy time of it or hard, it is entirely possible, and dare I say probable, that you will experience what I can only describe as Fudge Brain, long after the health visitors and flowers have gone and your infant has become a toddler, a pre-schooler and an independent offspring.

The good news is that there is an antidote to this fudgy state, which is Clarity Brain, in which you have such a surge of satisfaction and power, hormonally charged of course, that your brain becomes super-focused, super-sharp, and which, if you aren't careful, can make you feel as if Superwoman is a bit of a wimp because you are On the Case Completely.

Being a parent deprives you of so much time that it can bring out the best in the most disorganised person, it can make you focus with an intensity you did not think possible.

You only ever revisit your old life after you have a child; you will never re-enter it fully because your child has invaded your psyche and your soul permanently. Even when you are immersed in something else, whether it be sex or statistics, your attention is always a moment away from being shattered by a call or a thought or simply a child-related deadline.

Fudge Brain is really when you zone out in spite of yourself, when your thoughts turn inwards, away from the world of meetings and deadlines and responsibility and towards personal minutae.

I was in Fudge Brain during much of my first pregnancy, abandoning myself to the forty-week countdown. I was probably substantially less effective at my job from the moment I saw the appearance of the thin blue line announcing that I was pregnant.

Working women who work right up to the wire in their pregnancies get a huge shock because all the business of doing, planning, and organizing suddenly stops and is taken over by something else, or by someone else: your baby. Fudge Brain came and went after my children were born and as any parent knows, can and does return. Sometimes it is provoked by sleep deprivation, but at other times it is simply stress or change in a child or something happening to them at school. Whatever it is, it can mean that you feel like you are faking it in meetings because while your body may be in the room, your spirit or soul is definitely somewhere else.

 TOP TIP

Choose at least one way of staying connected to the non-baby world or risk feeling alienated when you resurface.

The only way to deal with this is to acknowledge it and work around it – make up for a fudge brain day with harder work the next.

Sally, forty-four, is an infant feeding co-ordinator. Her husband, Marcus, is a gardener who also practises Shiatsu massage. They have two daughters, aged thirteen and eleven.

When the girls were tiny we both worked part-time, me as a midwife and Marcus as a care worker. When I was offered a great opportunity to do something that really fascinated me, it seemed the natural thing for Marcus to work around school hours so that I did not have to worry about rushing home. I quite often have to go to conferences or have late meetings, and it is great to know that Marcus is there with the girls, leaving me completely free to concentrate on what I'm doing.

I have had to learn to let go. This means not minding when I come in through the door on a Friday with the weekend ahead that the house is a tip, or feeling irritated that things have not been done in the way I would have done them. If I had been at home, there would have been a sense of some sort of preparation for the weekend. You have to be disciplined about letting go of those feelings and remembering how lucky you are to have such a responsible partner.

It took some adjustment for Marcus, too and for a while he felt a bit unconfident, being so much in charge of everything. He would want to ring me to consult me about every detail. Now that his confidence has grown, I think he feels really proud of doing such a good job, knowing that the girls are doing so well at school, are really happy and well balanced. That's mostly down to him now.

Clear as a Bell

Hormones, like the Lord, work in mysterious ways. After our daughter Anoushka was born my mind seemed to be as clear as a bell. Clarity Brain was kicking in. Whereas I had felt distinctly over-whelmed as a first-time mother, after my second baby was born I felt I could swim the Channel, redesign the business, decorate the house, and reduce to a size twelve without the aid of surgery – and that was just in the first month.

I don't think you ever know what mental state you will be in after giving birth, any more than you can predict what kind of child you have. It is a fact of life that, just as one tiny yumpster will sleep and slurp quite happily, another will be not only awfully spotty and ugly but a screamer to boot; equally the mummy brain may be razor sharp or total fudge.

Within a couple of months of the birth of our youngest child, I had such a sudden surge of Clarity Brain that I rather rashly decided to set in motion the plans for my business, Editorial Intelligence, which I had been planning in my head for years. Up until the second I made the decision, I thought I had decided something else entirely, which was to become a home-based consultant, always at the school gates at 9.30 and 3.30. But I woke up one morning and thought: this is it. I have to do it, and I have a plan about how.

Even so, I started to base my new business at home, complete with one member of staff recruited through the babysitting network. I was convinced that I would have perfect work–life balance; I kidded myself that I was still being 'there', you see.

> ### ☛ TOP TIP
> Don't gear everything around your children and their needs, make them realize yours too. Give them consistency and cuddles, but let them cope with disappointment and complexity – just like you do.

One day we were about to send out our first big mailshot to clients. Wolfie, then aged six months, inched over on his bottom to the pile of letters and began to nibble at the stamps and dribble over the corners. Pretty soon we looked like an advert for

TOP TIP

Don't give it all up to be with your kids without planning financially a decade or so ahead; it will not be possible for you to re-enter the labour market 'just like that'.

toilet rolls with a human puppy adorably ruining all our hard work and an expensive mass mailing going straight into the bin. The following week I relented and rented an office locally and went back to work in a more traditional way.

CASE STUDY

Mary-Ann, a writer and broadcaster, has two teenage girls.

My life with small children was transformed when we worked out how to get a lie-in at weekends.

What we did was to ration the amount of TV the children (then aged about five and four) were allowed to watch during the week, but we told them they could watch for as long as they liked on Saturday and Sunday mornings as long as they didn't wake us up. So they learned to tiptoe downstairs, shut the sitting room door and turn on the telly. Result! We had two decent nights' sleep a week and were much less crotchety with them at the weekends.

From the earliest years of parenthood, we have insisted on spending one week a year doing 'we time' – on holiday without children. It is a way of nurturing our own relationship, and this precious week has become like an annual second honeymoon.

The children don't mind much, and we told them that, in return for having one week a year on our own, we'd be much nicer parents for the other fifty-one (quite true). They have managed perfectly well with a combination of nanny and granny. We'd seen so many couples split up after the children left home because their own relationship had shrivelled to a husk, having been mediated only through the children. An annual week a year on your own is a great protection from that.

Not So Wicked Stepmother

I have mentioned my stepchildren Rachael and Max and how my life as a single businesswoman in my early thirties, who thought that organizing dry cleaning was the height of domesticity (as, to some extent, I still do), was replaced overnight, thanks to them, by one of energy, company, chaos, mess, muddle, and warmth.

Having stepchildren was a really helpful practice run before my own were born. I can't imagine what it is like to have your first baby and not have around someone experienced who can say, 'Oh, you don't need to bother with stairgates, kids just bounce when they fall,' as Alaric did. Or to miss inheriting a whole library of well-worn books so you don't have to start from scratch. Or to not know what makes young children giggle (tickles) or feel grown up (late-night telly) or special (good spreads on birthdays).

Rachael and Max have always lived with us for half the week and half the holidays. They were eight and six when Roman was born ten years ago. Now that they are in their late teens, we are planning to seriously upgrade the perks to keep attracting them both on our annual fortnightly holiday together. I know there are stories of kids who put glue in their stepmum's knickers and worse (is there anything worse?) but I can't oblige on that front. Apart from a handful of testy moments, I have loved every minute of their company.

TOP TIP

Don't let guilt make you a martyr. No one wins if you try to make up for the time when you are out of the house by acting like a whirling dervish when you are back home again. Your children end up spoiled and lazy, and you end up more exhausted

These are my ideas for balancing your See-Saw if you have stepchildren.

First, remember that to them, no matter how well you get on, you are only second best. I have always had a good relationship with my stepchildren's mum, Lesley. Once in the early days, when I took the children swimming, Rachael stood in the dressing room, saying, 'You can't tell me what to do, you aren't my mum.' By totally fluky coincidence, Lesley was in the same place at the same time. She popped her head over the curtain and said, 'She may not be your mum, but I am, so do as Julia says.' I am always grateful for that moment of solidarity.

Second, give real, heartfelt attention to all your children, even if it can't be wholly equal. When Rachael and Max were still at primary school I drove them there on the way to my office. Although it meant that I often missed taking my little ones to nursery, it allowed me to demonstrate to my steppies that they also mattered to me when they could clearly see how besotted I was with the babies. This is important. Jealousy is real and so is insecurity.

I could not pretend there was 'no difference' between the way I felt about the children I grew from scratch and those I only got to know when they had been in the world, living with their real mum, for several years, but bonding time makes an impact. In the car I used to casually play new albums I'd bought that I thought they'd like and we'd drive in amiable silence, while I also managed to establish that Justin Timberlake and Gorillaz were cool (at least in the early noughties) and that I must not even *think* about putting on James Taylor because Max would be *sick*.

CASE STUDY

Jane, forty-seven, is a businesswoman with four teenage children. She lives with her partner, Hugh, an art gallery owner.

If I think I'm doing pretty well and am feeling very pleased about the day, all I have to do is go home and any ego I have is crushed against the nearest wall. Almost every time I open my mouth, I am called either 'a freak' or 'a weirdo'. Try keeping your self-esteem when you get that every time you try to ask an interesting question or be amusing. The children also wince when they catch a glimpse of your naked flesh or nearly gag at the sight of your ancient, gnarled feet.

It is almost impossible to be a pompous or self-satisfied bore if you have teenagers because they will take every opportunity to bring you down, like a pack of hyenas with an old lioness. They are simply not impressed by your life, so there's no point in trying to impress them, as you will only sound pathetic. I found myself desperately crying out, 'I've got a bloody degree, you know!' while they rolled around on the floor sniggering. When Hugh is going on a bit about art or literature or something, I am secretly relieved when the whole pack of them bring him down, too.

Presence, Not Presents

TOP TIP

Try and buy more time for your children rather than objects. An hour of actual attention is emotionally worth thousands of pounds to them.

One aspect that I think I have consistently got wrong as a parent is to confuse the giving of time with the giving of things. As a step-parent, I found it easier; I intentionally bought presents for Rachael and Max, not to assuage guilt but to show them really clearly that I valued them. In some circumstances money does talk. Young children who discover what it means to have their dad live with someone who isn't their mum need lots of reassurance.

Nevertheless, I'm not suggesting bribery here – I reserve that for my own children, whom I regularly palm off with the promise of some rubbish they have seen on the telly when my Slob Mum persona is fully in force. Not only do I usually regret this tactic later but the house is littered with clutter as a reminder.

Getting too many presents actually makes kids jumpy; there's the initial high when they receive a gift but there's also the inevitable low when they break it, or lose it, or see something else they want. This is not a comment about the consumer society, although I do feel a halo of smugness, of course, when the children play innocently and cheaply with a bit of string and some sticky-backed plastic, as we all do. No, you know exactly what I mean, I'm sure. It's just not a good idea to bribe or cajole or fob off your offspring with gifts, when all they want is *you*. It's far better to do what I have learned to do, which is sometimes to be present and correct, attentive,

TOP TIP

Do a time budget and work out if you are extended beyond your hourly means. Count up the hours you spend on work, travel and kids. Is this balance the best it can be?

and considerate. This means less guilt during the other times when I tune out, switch off, am tired or as grumpy as I feel, and let them... deal with it.

Landing on Planet Home from Planet Work

Time can seem too focused if you are a working parent. At some point you have to stop what you are doing, put on a different hat, and head for home. It is said that there is an epidemic of middle-class alcoholism caused by creeping over-indulgence in wine. I can believe it (even though I'm not really a drinker, more of a fooder). The traditional way of 'winding down' from the day has always been alcohol. I like the idea of a 'highball' myself: it has echoes of whatever men drank out of heavy, cut-glass tumblers in 1950s homes, and sounds as if it either made you relax or literally knocked you out. And, frankly, after a hard day at the office, or in traffic, or being pelted with email, or suffering God knows what kind of tedium or stupidity from life, we want something to knock us out, don't we, if we are honest?

But modern life means being responsible most of the time, so we are constantly striving for self-improvement and general betterment. I'm sure we are fascinated by the downward spiral of wayward celebrities like Amy Winehouse because they live out our irresponsibility for us while we get on with being Goody Two-Shoes.

Pooey Nights

For parents, the minute the day job ends the night job begins. This applies whether you leave your desk and go downstairs into family life, or whether you step out of an office door and step in through your front door. If your children are young, you can come home from work to a stint that ends, if you are lucky, at 8 p.m. but in reality is more like 9 or 10 p.m. if they are between about seven and twelve years old. Small wonder

TOP TIP

Plan buffer time between the end of work and home. Recognise it's a culture shock to walk in with a head full of office politics.

that we often delay our return home by unconsciously 'overrunning'. I once had a huge row with Alaric after I was out several nights in a row and he accused me – rightly – of missing what he called 'the shit shift': those term-time, post-supper hours when you are doing well if you get to bedtime without someone crying.

Re-Entry Problems

You aren't off the hook without children, though, because there is Gym Time, or Networking Time, or some other kind of time, which, on reflection, is a duty of some kind, albeit self-imposed. But the net effect is the same: vital wind-down time is lost. It needs to be regained because we have clipped out a moment *in between* work and home.

My friend Ella is recently back at work three days a week after having a baby. She has an emotionally draining job, work-ing with sick children. She now stays in Starbucks for 'at least half an hour, with a peppermint tea' before coming home to her son, to clear her head of what has happened during the day. This is sensible and essential.

TOP TIP

Walk home from work, even if it is miles away. By the time you get home, you will have got rid of all the office stuff and be ready to be bombarded with the demands of home.

My version of 're-entering

TOP TIP

Take your children to your office, show them your website: engage them in what you do.

the family atmosphere', as I call it, is to put on some really silly music as I come out of the tube, and then, just before I get to my road, put in a call to a girlfriend for a chat. I generally ring Jessica or Nina in New York, who are just about hitting lunchtime on the East Coast when I ring and are happy to talk. I loiter in the road, yakking for a few minutes, just before turning the key in the lock and hearing the wonderful but over-whelming sound, 'Mummeeeee!'

Arriving back at Planet Home is to arrive into a different physical and psychological place from work. Even though managing overload at work is difficult, it is nothing compared to the unpredictability of home. Some nights I return to calm order, the children happily munching, or goggling the box, or splashing in the bath, or playing. At other times I am met by a horde of needy, screaming banshees, baying at me angrily, hurling themselves at me for attention. There is no etiquette, just ordinary human behaviour without the social conventions of the workplace, where we might seethe about being unnoticed or overlooked, but hardly ever express anger or upset.

Dedicated Parenthood

If you don't want to work, as is becoming more of a trend – particu-

TOP TIP

Have a 'do nothing' day of holiday or unpaid leave once every six months to recharge, not to do chores.

larly in households where the frazzle factor becomes so im-mense that the emotional and financial costs just don't add up any more, then you face other difficulties. Get-ting a career back

62

on track after an extended break can be more hellish than escaping the nine to five. But keeping your hand in work if you are home-based is really possible only if you work for a large corporation that has the scale to support part-time working meaningfully, or are in the creative industries: in other words, if you freelance from home.

CASE STUDY

Annabelle, a mother of three children, is a freelance consultant in the social sector.

I am in the fortunate position not to be the main breadwinner and to work for myself, so I can work as much or little as I want. I worked about 75 per cent of my time before my third child arrived. That was too much for me. I wondered why I was putting in such long hours while somebody else was looking after my kids when I did not need the money. I vowed to work only 50 per cent of my time, but soon found it was creeping up beyond that. I have just now subcontracted someone else to keep my hours down. The ideal is working just school hours. Then you are there for the kids before and after school, as well as during most of the holidays.

Sometimes I am jealous of my friends with children who have more ambitious careers, but in many cases their high-profile, full-time job is at the expense of time with their children, and no doubt they look at me longingly. These friends have excelled in the workplace because they are the main breadwinners, but had they been in my situation of having a high-earning husband, they probably would have opted for less demanding work. On balance, I feel very lucky.

Another key success factor is being able to afford quality help. I have someone who does ten hours of cleaning per week as well as a nanny who looks after the kids when I am working. So when I am not working, I don't have to spend my whole time on household duties, but can instead play with the kids. Because of the time I do spend with them, I don't feel guilty when I am not there, even when they try to make me!

There are clear advantages to full or near full-time parenthood of small children – an unmatched deliciousness in the way they see the world and take pleasure from the smallest things – but you have to step back completely from the speedy, competitive, full-on culture of work in order to do it. I'm not surprised that, at least on a temporary basis, those who give up work rather than work part-time seem more relaxed emotionally than those tearing off their work hat to put on their home hat. I watch Alaric and Wolfie go round the house with the vacuum cleaner, or making pastry together, or chatting, *mano a mano*, in utter bliss, and I'm grateful for the generational leap that has made this possible. But Alaric knows he has made, not a temporary sacrifice for the children, but more like a complete career sacrifice, which started eighteen years ago when his first child was born and his then partner, like me, was the main wage earner.

If I could design a template for the least worst option in the first eighteen years of your child's life, it is probably to be self-employed with plenty of money set aside for contingencies, some savings, and income protection in place, coupled with a flexible approach that suits you and your clients or employer equally well, so that you can be involved with your children's term and holiday time as much as possible without feeling like a split personality, trying to be consumed by and ever-present at both. A friend who read this said wistfully, 'That sounds idyllic.' Sadly for most of us it is just that: an ideal that is not yet a reality.

Pyjama Parties at Eight O'Clock

Since I work during the day and miss out on such a lot at home, we often have a little one in the bed with us. There are few things more relaxing than drifting off with the fat arm of a toddler around your neck as he sleepily talks through his day. It is also a good way to have the odd early night, because some evenings after a bath and a snuggle at 8 p.m. I forget to resurface. I care for none of the disapproval that could well go with this – ranging from complaints about three-year-olds not sleeping in their own beds to them needing one of us next to him in order to go to sleep. What I'm doing in this moment is making the best of the time I do have with my little one, and he loves it too. In fact sometimes he is aggrieved if I am clearly going downstairs again instead of staying put. 'Why aren't you in your jim-jams too, Mummy?' he asks sternly.

On nights when I actually am an adult who has an evening ahead of her, we talk about why he can't have me on demand as he would like and it kind of clears the air for a little person denied my company (and me his) for most of each weekday. 'I don't like it when you leave the house,' he'll say and I reply, 'I know, but I have to, now let's have a cuddle and you can tell me all about nursery,' which is a good compromise. It's not a perfect result for him, but it's Good Enough, a phrase I'd like to enshrine above the door of every person on the See-Saw: when one priority goes up another comes down. This book is all about gentler landings, not fantasy changes.

Quality Time

Don't you loathe the phrase 'quality time' just because it is so perfect? I mean, how can we improve on the description? Children don't want lots of time with you so much as they want special time with you. As my life coach would say, they want you to be 'fully present'. Being there in the room and there in spirit are, of course, very different things. I am often in cyberspace in my head and home in North London in person; or I'm physically on the sofa but I'm snoozing, or reading, or most definitely tuning out.

This is OK up to a point. As a friend said of our brilliant babysitter, 'She is paid to be attentive.' And as mums and dads we know that we can get away with being less whatever it is than paid help, just because we can. We know we are loved come what may and who doesn't exploit that sometimes? I know I do (Meany Mum). However, just as you can repress the need to exercise until you find you have bits of your body meeting your knees that should be way, way higher, you can ignore your kids only for so long without consequences. We all know the signs when children feel neglected, or parcelled out, either too much or at a time that is hard for them. These include rudeness, tearfulness, sibling aggression, and general disobedience well above acceptable levels.

Of course, if you have limited time with the family, you may think you have to be with all the children, all of the time. Mistake. Big Mistake. Huge. Because this is an invitation to fail for everyone. Children become like puppies scrambling over themselves for a piece of Mummy action, while Mummy shrinks back into the corner, thinking: get me outta here.

The solution is quality time *one-to-one*. You have to get counter-intuitive at this point. Don't throw this book down and mutter in despair about it not being possible. Think it through. You may have no partner, no childcare, and two kids. It is still possible, albeit with negotiation and possibly bribery of one child, to have time on your own with the other. You have to agree between you what you will do. If possible, you make a regular slot, a ring-fenced time.

TOP TIP

Let children learn to amuse themselves and avoid over-scheduling activity for them: it's exhausting to organize for you and often draining for them after school.

But if that isn't possible, it is still OK to just make sure they know you want to be with them on their own.

Sometimes my children do brilliant impersonations of spoiled, grabby, I want-ers who could easily feature on a TV nanny show and win Worst Brat Award. Nevertheless, they generally do that only when one of us isn't paying serious attention to them and giving them any quality time. No amount of reading and playing by themselves compensates children for what they also need regularly: one-to-one time with an adult of their choice.

On the whole when I do plan so that I can spend an hour or two alone with one of my offspring, they don't want me to buy them anything or berate me; they want to talk, or show me something, or draw with me, or do something utterly (a) delightful and (b) cheap, and we end up having a great time. Every Friday afternoon I pick up Anoushka from school and we drive to the same place to window-shop, buy crêpes, and go visiting. Every Saturday morning I take Wolfie to one of those council-run padded cells for children with indoor slides that he calls 'runny jumpy'. Every Sunday I take Roman out by himself. Sometimes we get no further than the local coffee shop, a favourite, but other times we go further afield and take in some culture together.

Bunking Off School

When I was at school in the 1970s we would call playing truant 'bunking off'. Nowadays if you take your children out of school without permission, the head teacher has the right to take your misdemeanour to the local authority, which can in theory prosecute you. Teachers swear that if children troop in and out of school at whim, going on extended holidays, it interrupts lessons and is a nightmare.

But I wish I could treat my children the way I treat myself: to a day off when I need it; to balancing doing paperwork with creative brainstorming and planning; to adjusting and adapting to the real rhythm of my concentration. It is not ideal to operate like a machine, fully 'on' for extended hours and even days at a time. So I'd like to decide to have a long weekend and take the children out on a Friday or Monday without having to get written permission first. Or even to judge whether one of the children might be better off having a quiet few days at home reading, and having space to think. My sister-in-law home-educates her two sons from a houseboat on the Thames, which is perfectly legal, but once you're inside the school system there is zero flexibility, which is a real shame.

Policymakers are supposed to be getting more flexible, encouraging people to work in completely different shift patterns to ease the burden in all sorts of ways, but schools are still run totally at odds with this thinking. They finish in the middle of the day when parents are still at work and although plans are in place for 'wraparound' breakfast clubs and after-school care, it is not clear how widespread this will be, nor, frankly, how well thought through and enjoyable.

I think that schools need to think practically about how the way they run affects not just the well-being and exam results of children inside school hours, but outside, too. I really wish local education authorities would abandon their rigid, all-inclusive policy on absenteeism, which treats all parents and kids as if they are advocating truancy if they want time off in term-time, and instead ask head teachers and, if necessary, governors to use their judgement and discretion about what is acceptable for each child. I also wish that parents' evenings and sports days could be scheduled at different times to suit office-based families as well as the home-based.

For my part I know that forward planning all dates, including the dreaded 'inset' days for teacher training, is essential if you want to stand a chance of not missing an assembly. But I have practically given up trying to be available in the middle of the afternoon for what is mistermed parents' evenings, and tend to make appointments with teachers one-to-one. Luckily our primary school is very well managed, with good co-ordination and co-operation between the teachers, the office staff, and the parents, which makes life a lot easier.

Family Supper

There is no such thing as breakfast in our house, only DIY cereal and toast, with the occasional serving of porridge. But a proper cooked meal at suppertime is on the menu and Family Supper, which we try to do once a week, is everyone's favourite. If you are serious about wanting to avoid the sense of disconnection that comes from working hard and being on the See-Saw, then you have to make time for Family Supper. And yes, you have to be more Jamie Oliver than ready-meal about it. Real food, cooked from scratch. No one can say it isn't quick enough any more, thanks to Nigella, Nigel et al.

What we don't manage in our family, which I always intend

> ☞ **TOP TIP**
> Give children chores and teach them to do their bit, but don't expect them to do them as well as you.

to do, is involve the children more in the cooking, table laying, and clearing up. This is because it's actually easier and quicker to do it all yourself. But children love being given tasks as long as you have started them off early enough in life before slob rot starts setting in.

Alaric makes incredible homemade pizza, which goes down a treat (and no, he isn't available on loan, and yes, he's still an ordinary man who gets grumpy despite doing a good impersonation in this book of being utterly heroic). My favourite photo is of him in our kitchen on Anoushka's birthday, cutting a pizza into slices with all the children leaning forward hungrily.

'Are we having family supper?' the children will ask. And if we nod the reaction is the same: 'Yessss!'

The Love Sandwich

Some months after my friend Tanya had her baby, her eldest child said casually, 'I'm bored with the baby now, Mummy. Can we put him in the bin?' which roughly translates as: 'I'm *soooo* jealous.' Similarly, Roman was so upset about Anoushka's birth – he was two and a half – that he climbed into her wicker cot and capsized it, giving himself a big bruise as he landed. He looked like he felt: wounded by jealousy.

Jealousy and children go together like bread and Marmite, or biscuits dipped in milk: they are a hard combination to break. I have a quick recipe for dealing with the awful sibling puppy-brawls that can break out around me, which is to make a game of cuddling in which we all pile together in a great big squeezy love sandwich. If you can add a few pillows into the equation, so much the better. Then you start identifying who is what in the love sandwich, which child is the bread, the cheese, or the honey. Soon they forget why they hate

TOP TIP

Set boundaries for your children and don't break them out of guilt that you aren't around enough.

each other and start to enjoy the game. It takes only five minutes and it doesn't always work, of course, but more often than not it does.

RECIPE

RECIPE: KID CAPPUCCINO

TIME: One or two hours per week at the same time.

INGREDIENTS: One child, one adult.

For some reason children think coffee is the height of glamour. Well, mine do. They are always lobbying for a sip of cappuccino. I started to take out my eldest son Roman regularly on Sundays. We have a ritual: he brings his homework folder and we walk up the hill to the nearest Caffè Nero where we sit together, ostensibly to go through his homework but mainly to chat while I drink coffee. Although he tries to drink my coffee too, he actually has an orange juice, and we watch another loyalty stamp get filled in. It's very satisfying, reasonably healthy, and puts a big tick in the 'quality time' box. And, of course, the coffee is good, too.

5

Damned by the 'Dammy'

Have you ever heard of Mayzie the lazy bird? She flies away to the sunshine way off in Palm Beach, having tricked loyal, faithful Horton the elephant to look after her egg, but she wants it back when all the hard work is done. Luckily, Horton is a creation of the marvellous Dr Seuss, so his reward for all that egg childcare is for an ele-bird to fly out of the eggshell looking less like a bird and more like his ele-carer instead!

Mothers who leave their kids with loyal men can feel very disloyal. They can feel undeserving. And they can feel usurped. Don't be shocked, but my children often call me Dad by mistake, even though I'm there as often as not at bathtime and bedtime, and even though I'm there all weekend. They each do it, regularly. Typically, they correct themselves halfway through a sentence: 'Dad, can I have...? I mean, Mum, can I have some crisps?' I know I said I wear the trousers, but that's not why they call me Dad. It's because Alaric is the one who collects them from school most days, not me. He is the one they are hard-wired to turn to in the hours I cannot be there.

CASE STUDY

Phillipa, forty, an advertising executive, lives with her partner Dave who looks after their children, aged six and seven.

I have always made the money and so when we first considered getting together we worked out that Dave would be the one to stay at home.

It's been much more difficult than we thought because we had the kids very close together. So Dave was really up against it and felt very frazzled. I responded by getting him help, in the form of a nanny share, so he could have some time off. However, he also found that really difficult, I think because he felt that I was telling him that he should get it together to do something else as well as looking after the kids, and it made him go into some sort of defensive meltdown.

It has settled down now and he has taken some courses that have interested him while the kids have been at school. Of course, we do sometimes argue about the way things have turned out. He can be a bit of a moaner and I feel that in a way he has so much more freedom than me because I am absolutely stuck with being the breadwinner. Dave still doesn't really know what he wants to do and we can't seem to work out a plan so that things could change while we could also survive financially.

Our local nursery, Archway Under Fives, has noticed an increase in men who, as the head Nasso Christou puts it, 'share the care'. Certainly every man I know without exception organizes his life around his family in a way that would have been unthink-

TOP TIP

Separate out your priorities for your Dammy. Sort organizational jobs like play dates or outings from developmental goals like lots of lego playing.

able a generation ago. I once asked two single men for supper at our house, only for them to decline politely because, as separated parents, they wanted to spend precious time with their children.

Alaric is highly unusual because he is a proper dammy – a dad who fulfils the mum's traditional role. During the week he does all the shopping, washing, cleaning, and cooking, whilst I work mostly conventional hours in an office. He is the short-order chef when the children want spicy wraps for their supper, and when they want to find the T-shirt that they must wear this morning they ask him, because generally he bought it, washed it, and put it away, not me.

When we first got together, we talked a lot about how we would share childcare and household chores. He had been doing the dammy role with his big children, Rachael and Max, and he just said to me one day, as we were walking in the park and talking about our future together, 'I'll be the one who stays at home, and you can go out and have the career, because that will work out best.'

TOP TIP

Let your Dammy be better than you at some things – enjoy it. Treat it like delegating – celebrate it being done well.

Tim, thirty-six, is a painter and decorator. His wife, Sharon, is the manager of a leisure centre. They have three children aged fifteen, thirteen, and eleven. Three years ago Tim became what he calls a 'house-hubby'.

When Sharon got this great new job at a newly built leisure centre, we both sat down and realistically looked at how on earth we would manage with the three kids. Up until then, Sharon had been working part-time at another leisure centre but they saw her potential and the job she was offered was full time. At first she wanted to turn it down because she felt she would be unhappy with the long hours required.

I asked her who was the next best person to take care of the kids and she said that it was me, of course. The prospect excited me and the kids were old enough for me to work during school hours anyway. I feel very proud of what she had achieved because she started having kids quite young (we were both nineteen when she got pregnant) and yet that hasn't seemed to hold her back.

I have really got to know the kids these past few years and it has made our relationship so much stronger. They always used to turn to Sharon if they wanted something but now they tend to ask me if they want help of some kind. Without this arrangement, it's possible I might have been a bit cut off from them, the way my own dad was.

Green Eyes

Alaric was both right and wrong. In some ways it has worked out perfectly and certainly I am the envy of a number of women who see our set-up. But I have felt intense jealousy over the years and, of course, I have felt guilt. I have felt that I 'ought' to be the one with the children or that he is somehow preventing me from playing my full maternal role because I 'have' to be the main breadwinner.

But then Alaric is often jealous of me because no matter how many of the basic chores he does, the children always fling themselves at me when I walk in from work, always want my attention and, when I'm there and they are cut or hurt, they will go to me first. No amount of the closeness that men achieve with their children seems to break their bond with a mum, and I'm grateful for that. I can't help it: I do want to be wanted most. I sometimes find I'm competing with my own husband to feel 'the best' parent and this is pure See-Saw stuff: wanting to have my cake and eat it.

CASE STUDY

Laura, thirty-eight, is a garden designer with two children aged eight and ten. She is married to Robin, a builder.

Five years ago I decided that I wanted to study garden design. In order to afford this, I worked as a childminder and also took my course, which meant asking Robin to be around much more than he had been. I thought it was fine to ask him particularly as he had always been pushing to have children and was very focused on being a family man.

I have to say it was the most difficult patch of our marriage because the arrangement seemed to tip things out of kilter. It really took me by surprise. Despite himself, and despite saying that he wanted to support me and also that he enjoyed being with the kids, he seemed to really resent me. Perhaps it was because I was doing something new and he was still doing the same work. He became

Mary Poppins

If you have ever had to drop off a young child at nursery or with a childminder, leaving them screaming with indignation at best, or in a state of utter loss and panic at worst, or if you've had to rush away from work to collect them, you will know that there are times when the work–life stress seems almost unbearable.

Leaving your child in someone else's care can feel – not all the time, but sometimes and often unexpectedly – like a kind of profound loss, a process that is invisible to everyone except the person experiencing it, and acknowledged in a sympathetic but 'get-on-with-it' kind of way.

Even leaving your child with its father doesn't necessarily protect you from this feeling.

 TOP TIP

Don't automatically say how stressed and tired you are. Balance it with something positive about your work because it sends those signals to your children.

Betina, forty-one, is an account manager in a publishing house, with two children aged four and five. She is married to Drew, an importer of Italian food.

I love my children, I really do, but it really didn't suit me being at home with them all the time. I became a bit depressed by the relentless routine at home and so was thrilled to be approached by my ex-boss a year ago with the offer of a new job.

We are lucky in that we have managed to find a nanny who picks up the younger child from nursery and collects the older one from school. I actually think she is better than me at thinking of fun things for them to do, and she has a whole group of nanny friends whom she seems to really like hanging out with at the swings. It is awful to admit but the kids seem happier now that she is around because she is so much jollier and very hearty in that Australian way.

In the new job I really felt myself fitting back into my old perception of myself but I can't pretend that Drew's family didn't make me feel that I was being a bit of a crap mother. There were more than a few comments along the lines of 'I don't know how you can bear being away from them' or 'Don't you worry that something is going to happen to them and you won't be there?' Well, no. Sorry. I am a much better mother now because I am fulfilling all those different sides of myself. When I was at home, picking brown bits of Play-Doh off the floor, I did think: is this why I worked so hard? I became a bit of a mope and cut myself off from the kids. Now when I am with them, I am much more engaged.

Off Duty

One of the hardest things for me about leaving the children to go to work is that I give up the power to direct how things are done. I have to cede control to whoever is in charge, whether that is a babysitter or the children's dad. Yet it can be completely maddening to come home at 9 p.m. and find my kids not just still awake but watching some grisly bit on *Midsomer Murders*. Or I may simply find that in the space of a few nights I am out of sync with their routine, and have to remind myself that I can't just jump in and start running the house as I would like.

The truth is that working mothers are not always in 'Mother Knows Best' positions of superiority. One of the prices we pay for working full time, still trapped in the largely inflexible nine-to-five working model, is to realize that we have a major role in our children's lives *but it is not the only major role.*

It makes me feel queasy just writing this, because I love my children so much that I cannot bear the thought of not being the most important person to them, but why should I be? Isn't the most stable and happy child one who is sure of who loves them, and who feels secure in themselves? The best thing I can do as a working mum is to not come home and make a fuss, acting as if they have lost something by my being out of the house. If I really feel that, maybe I should think what that means and do something about it. No, the truth is that I have to do what we all do, all day long on the See-Saw: get on with it, and sometimes bite the blanket in anguish when no one is looking.

On the See-Saw: David

A charity programme head, David works from Monday to Thursday in London and goes home to Wales at the weekends to his wife, Anne, who is twenty-seven weeks pregnant, and their daughter, aged two.

We have just had a marital tiff because I broke one of the rules of our See-Saw: no logistical conversations in the evening. It started because I wanted the extra financial help to start now rather than after the birth of the new baby. My wife, worn out by a humid day with our two-year-old daughter, Beatrice, insisted that three weeks after the birth was fine, which was of no comfort. The fact that the argument was more about me, trying to assuage my guilt and frustration at being absent in Central London from Monday through Thursday at this stage of her pregnancy, is of less comfort still.

We've had this weekly split existence for eighteen months now and have been learning the rules of the road. When it works it can be fabulous, but it relies on vigilance in following our 'rules' and having sufficient back-up. During Anne's current pregnancy there have been too many instances when we have been on very thin ice.

The pattern of our weeks and our 'rules' have evolved more through experience than design; it has often taken a Sunday-evening meltdown to prompt reflection and change. However, I attempt to make sense of my week by splitting it into four distinct areas framed by the Paddington–Cardiff train journey: relationship; family; work; and me.

Our Friday-night date à deux is a non-negotiable anchor. Most importantly, our 120 per cent trustworthy regular babysitter cuts us loose at 7.30 p.m. Anne puts on heels, we hold hands, walk to a local restaurant, and talk. I like reconnecting emotionally and physically with Anne before the differently magical, Saturday-morning patter of feet *and the cry of 'Daddy!'*

From Monday to Thursday I have a heady freedom: I can work earlier or later; I can do evening networking without the tug of the bedtime story. I can see friends, catch up on sleep, swim, or meditate. In all of this I follow religiously a routine of morning and evening telephone calls to Anne. Also, I ensure that I do not make the mistake (as I often have) of packing my week in London to capacity so that I arrive in Wales spent at the weekend. I need to get home with medium to high energy so I can give Anne her 'day off' on the Saturday and do the night cover without becoming an irritable zombie.

I have taken a job where I can have 'clean' weekends: no work happens. This feels odd as well as vaguely decadent, and it is the first time this has happened in my professional life (probably due to my failure to purge my persistent Protestant work ethic). But it means that when I am with Anne and Beatrice, I am fully present. When we all lived under the same roof the whole week, I was physically there every evening but too often emotionally absent.

Sunday nights range from bitter-sweet to traumatic. Following bathtime, all is fine if I head to the station leaving Anne reading Alfie *to a sleepy Beatrice. I feel a wrench but also a sense of relaxation as I head into the Severn Tunnel, a glass of red wine to hand. However, if I leave a coughing Beatrice who has passed on the latest bug to an exhausted Anne, I am filled with guilt and regret. On occasion I push my departure back until the Monday train at 5.15 a.m.*

From the London Eye to Penarth Pier can feel a long way. Sometimes the geography can enable a clearer focus to the activities of the week, making them all the more satisfying, rather than my spending my energy trying to juggle them all at once and succeeding in none. At other times, a three-and-a-half-hour dash to the emergency room at the hospital, while calls to my mobile are constantly redirected into my voicemail, can be testing.

I think we quickly realized that there is no ideal; there are too many variables. I guess we strive to be as vigilant as we can of what works for our particular dynamics and those of our family relationships at given moments in time, while trying to refine them and pick up tips along the way.

However, if you're in the same situation, never be put off by a two-hour train journey. A seat, the quiet carriage, the countryside, onboard food and wine, and, crucially, uninterrupted time can make everything else possible. The train is my sanity buffer.

6

Work and Childcare on the See-Saw

Thank God I'm not in politics. Thank God I don't have to try to unpick the hideous mess that passes for law in relation to equality, flexible working, maternity leave, paternity leave, and childcare. I became entangled in a horrible spaghetti of laws, amended laws, bills, regulations, and political plans when researching this chapter. Just when I felt vaguely on top of the situation, another fresh political commitment would come along and rejig what is on offer.

Politicians do try hard to get it right, but deep down they all know that whatever they promise to deliver there is no easy solution to the financial, emotional, and practical cost of both working and having children, whether you are employed, self-employed, unemployed, or an employer.

Childcare's Catch-22

Finding good local childcare ought to be as fundamental as having good local schools and hospitals, but right now it isn't. Lack of availability, lack of imagination and lack of funding all conspire to make under-five and pre-school provision messy and very hit-and-miss in terms of availability and quality.

And of course, nowadays the victory of sorting out childcare is offset by the huge stab of guilt about working at all when children are very young. Let's face it, society is completely confused about whether it thinks women should work after having babies. The government pledged in Autumn 2008 to extend free nursery places for two year olds to fifteen hours a week. This was met by a good deal of outrage in the media, with many saying, 'I thought good mothering was staying at home these days, why provide an incentive to go out to work?'

Well, the answer is simple: neccessity. Most people I know dearly wish they could spend more time at home with their young children, they dearly wish they could get off the rat race nine to five treadmill, but they can't. The fact that many like their work doesn't mean they want to do as much of it as they do. The current law tends to send people to the extremes of the See-Saw: either giving it all up because there isn't enough childcare to cover the cost of working or working too much in order to pay for any childcare at all.

> **☞ TOP TIP**
>
> Watch your children closely and listen to them. Are they telling you something about how they are finding their nanny / nursery / childminder that you aren't seeing because you don't want to? It is important to contemplate that you may not have the right solution and then change the circumstances, even if it plays havoc with work.

Janice, forty-four, a freelance editor with two teenage children, lives with her husband Paul in Manchester.

As soon as the kids were born I started working from home. With one foot on the bouncy chair, I would try to do my editing or writing work. Of course, this worked for brief periods when they were very tiny but as soon as they were up and about it got much harder.

Then I moved on to having a childminder, and there was a friend whose kid I looked after twice a week too, only in the morning though. So I just used to work whenever I could: when the kids were asleep, in the night-times, and sometimes early in the morning. That way I just about managed to make a half-decent living and be with the kids in the afternoons. When they got older I could meet them from school. That system of grabbing time worked for me. That's still how I work, except that I go into publishers' offices on a freelance basis, but I've really got used to hustling for work and meeting deadlines with my family life going on all around me. I couldn't work any other way now.

Ask anyone about childcare and you get some serious eye-rolling. There is always a story to tell, always a struggle to find it, afford it, keep it, manage the time slots. Over the course of the lives of our five children, every variation on a theme of childcare has been tried: nanny (she lasted a week when she realized Alaric actually used the kitchen and was in the house during the day – nannies like to rule their roost without annoying parents in the way); manny (a

☞ TOP TIP

If you work from home, create a separate 'office space', even if it is divided by supermarket boxes.

lovely Brazilian man hired from an after-school helper agency one summer who left almost immediately to become an actor); and nursery. We have experimented with full-time care, part-time, and none at all. What you gain in financial saving, you lose in precious time, and the wrong childcare, or not enough of it, is worse than none at all.

All our children stayed at home for the first nine months or so (with my husband as the live-in Dammy). As little as ten years ago there was no real debate about the 'dangers' of putting children in nursery for long hours. The problem wasn't wrestling with your conscience, it was wrestling with finding private nurseries to put them in and worrying about the standard of care when you did.

With the certainty of hindsight I know that the first nursery I put my eldest into wasn't great – there was a huge fuss over one particularly shouty carer – but even the others which gave excellent care did so in rigid hours of either just the morning or all day. I opted for all day and I regret it now, even though I know I didn't have much of a choice then and that most working parents have none at all if they want to pay the mortgage.

See-Saw Law

Despite the fact that the government *needs* you to work, *wants* you to work (it is an EU commitment to have 60 per cent of women working by 2010), and it spends huge amounts of money trying to tinker with legislation to help women and men go back to work flexibly, the first hurdle – after finding a good nursery with a place, or a nanny share, or a childminder – is the cost.

Whilst the law will entitle a woman to take up to a year off work by 2010, the reality for most women is that the sums just don't add up, even if they want to drop out completely from the work market for what is a very long time indeed (think how out of touch you feel after a holiday). The government does allow you to have ten 'Keeping in Touch' days during the thirty-nine weeks of Statutory Maternity Pay, but that's just a working fortnight out of more than half a year.

In terms of money, here are the numbers. For the first six weeks of maternity leave you are paid 90 per cent of any rate of salary. After that a new mother's source of income drops dramatically. For the next thirty three-weeks you get the standard rate of just over £100 per week (unless you earn less than £90 a week in the first place, in which case you would qualify for benefits). So, not surprisingly, most people feel they have to go back to work very soon after their baby is born, in order to cover their cost of living – which of course rises anyway with a new baby.

Quite where this sits with the increasing political noise about mothers and children being together lots and lots in the early years is beyond me. The cost of childcare in proportion to disposable income is simply way too high. Those Treasury bods, and all the other policy wonks who are trying to tighten up public finances, delude themselves that the rest of us have lots of spare money after paying the mortgage and all our other bills. In Britain it costs on average between £150 and £200 per week per child for either childminding or nursery places, which is between two to four times as much as in Finland, and up to eight times more than in Sweden. It is normal, yes, *normal*, for families in the UK to have to meet between 40 and 75 per cent of these costs, which is at least £5,000 a year per child after tax breaks and current subsidies, unless you qualify for larger amounts because you have very little or no fixed income.

So, you have your baby, you receive pretty much all your salary for the first six weeks, but then you have at least two more years (not counting the half a year at £100 Statutory Maternity Pay a week if you are a middle income earner) before you qualify for a handful of hours a week childcare and poorly subsidized childcare at that. It's a nasty catch-22 for everyone, not least because the economy needs more people earning and paying taxes, not fewer.

I would say that whichever political party sorts out a clear policy on what real working parenthood costs, and how to square this with the ideal of today's culture on spending as much time as possible with children when they are tiny, would be on to a landslide victory of votes.

CASE STUDY

Jessica, a communications consultant, has three children and lives in New York.

All the skills I need to parent – 24-hour patience, super-human time management, schizophrenia (from chairing board meetings in the city one minute to rushing home to help the five-year-old read), massive amounts of empathy, discipline, vigilance, physical and mental dexterity – are those needed in the workplace. Why is childcare not seen as management?

When I went for my first job in New York the chairman asked me about my management experience. I told him I could either bore him with tales of the workplace or show off about how happy my kids were after moving from London to New York, courtesy of moi. I explained I thought the latter was of greater relevance than the former. He guffawed. I got the job. If only we could be more proud...

Trapped in The System

So, welcome to the childcare lottery. The current system means that:

- You don't know until the last moment if, when and where you have a childcare place.
- Unless you qualify for benefits you are unlikely to get meaningful assistance to meet the cost.
- There is as much juggling involved in getting young babies and toddlers to and from nursery as a daily international commute.
- The cost of leaving the job market, if you decide to stay at home too long, is as high as going back to work earlier than you wish and staying connected to the workplace.
- Even if you work flexibly at the office this doesn't necessarily match with the flexible free hours offered by the nursery: the workplace doesn't join up to the nursery.

And, of course, the biggest irony of all is that everyone is too busy to do anything about changing the – dread word – *system*. I did briefly transform myself into an ardent campaigner one year when Islington Council tried to double Wolfie's nursery fees with a 'consultation', which was in effect a fait accompli. We started to complain very loudly at the eleventh hour, which was the earliest we understood what was going on.

I did all the things that instant campaigners do: I sat up all night pulling off information from the internet; I mobilized mums and dads and co-opted the local paper; I put up posters, wrote letters, lobbied councillors. I cajoled, threatened and ballooned in self-righteous indignation, because all the parents who, like

TOP TIP

Watch your health. It can be fine until your forties and then it can give you some shocks.

me, were going to have to unpick all their family finances or take their toddlers out of a nursery in which they were settled and happy, had right on their side. And so, at the eleventh hour and a bit, the council *did* actually back down in part and freeze the fees for existing parents. I was so exhausted from the instant campaign on top of everything else that as soon as my summer holiday began I collapsed in a heap with pneumonia and ended up in hospital. Looking on the bright side, at least I got some rest there and at least we could continue to send our boy to nursery.

CASE STUDY

Julia is a social campaigner and rabbi.

Expect childcare to cost a fortune in the first eight years. It cost me more than I earned. But it was worth it. I felt safe, the children felt safe, and we are still very good friends with their nanny, Joanna. Never stint on childcare. Have the best you can afford, and then some.

I'm constantly trying to get my life in order so that I can do everything. This means living with lists, but the problem is that I find myself waking in the night, knowing the balance of the See-Saw is wrong because I'm thinking of what's on the list. Work–life balance isn't unachievable, just difficult. Circumstances shift all the time so the pattern goes out of sync. Also, some events inevitably stretch the fairly fragile organization of things to breaking point. I'm thinking of sick parents in particular. So, at times it does feel more See-Saw than balanced, definitely, yes.

High-Street Nursery

I know a woman who put her baby on a waiting list for a nursery in the green belt outside London when she was still pregnant and he still didn't get in because the waiting list was so long. Some people in Britain may accept queuing – to get into a football match or Wimbledon, at the Harrods sale, on motorways – but not me. I especially detest the idea of being on a *waiting list* to get into childcare that isn't even especially affordable.

Friends of mine who run a private nursery told me in ghastly detail about all the hoops they had to jump through in setting up and running it, plus the costs involved. It's not just that they have to comply with more health and safety regulations than there are for a hospital and a restaurant combined: I'm in favour of that. But there is precious little incentive, support, or funding to help people start nurseries. If you're prepared to spend days, even weeks, scouring websites to find funding, apply and then sit on a waiting list for months while your application is on hold, fine. And if you want to raise venture capital to finance a nursery, by all means go ahead.

I'd like to see the corporate trend-setters – leaders in flexible working with modern workplaces, like BT, Vodafone, Lloyds TSB, and Sainsbury's, whose vast resources are channelled to provide products and in-store service – put the same energy and know-how into funding and being involved at a managerial level in high-street day care, in association with existing local-authority-funded nurseries.

Apart from a shortage of nurseries altogether, and apart from a shortage of affordable places, most nurseries lack the kind of flexibility that the private sector offers its consumers, because nurseries are heavily regulated and exclusively managed by the local council. If corporate businesses teamed up in association with those trained in childcare, we could see a revolution in availability as well as some

TOP TIP

When it comes to childcare, have a plan A, B, and C – and probably D, too.

dynamic changes in boring but vital things like shift patterns. Surely the parent who has to start work at 8 a.m. but finishes at 1 p.m. three days a week should be able to buy that amount of time in much the same way that you can buy a mobile phone tariff to suit you. In reality, most nurseries offer very few, very rigid time slots, so parents either leave their children in them longer than they would like, to cover for the one morning or afternoon a week for which they need 'long' cover, or they have a hole where provision should be.

In politics, public–private partnership money is used to fund academies and hospitals, with mixed results, but I want the private sector *know-how* as much as their money. As the situation currently stands, central government, whose example is followed by local authorities, dictates how consumers experience high-street childcare.

Wouldn't it be nice to know that we begin to have as much choice and control over our nursery provision as we do over how many types of soap we can buy, or suits we can choose?

CASE STUDY

Antonia, leader writer at the London *Evening Standard* and on the Conservative Party's candidate list, is a mother of three.

Exploit the fact that attitudes have changed towards working from home and part-time working. Hector Sants, chief executive of the Financial Services Authority, the City's leading regulator, often works from home one day a week. The organization says that option is available to all staff, informally if not contractually. That example from the top would have been rare in the City ten years ago. And if you can afford to go part-time, do. Yes, you often have to cram into three days what belongs in five, and get paid for only three, but the certainty of promising that you will make it to the school play or art show or football match because you are *definitely* not working that day is worth a lot.

I think men and women in professional jobs now are more open about the fact that they have family responsibilities, and that the back-up sometimes breaks down. About twelve years ago I remember an unexpected childcare crisis, which forced me into the park with the pushchair. That usually sent my son to sleep and, if it didn't, at least the wind noise would drown out any squeaks that would otherwise be audible to my interviewee over the phone. Desperate measures, really.

Nowadays, by contrast, people seem to be able to admit to the fact that they've got a childcare meltdown but are still making the calls. I always preferred a 6 or 7 a.m. start, and getting home early, to a later start with hours that ran on into the evening. I think in the morning children are too bleary and focused on breakfast to care much about your absence (provided their PE kit has made it into the games bag the night before). If you can, it's more important to be back home in good time in the afternoon or evening to help with homework and pick up the pieces of the day.

Nanny Tax

For those who know the nightmare of getting good nurseries, some prefer the nanny route. There seem to be two kinds of experiences. Those who feel the nanny has saved their lives, and who tend to keep the nannies for years and years, plying them with flats and cars and trips abroad as incentives. Then there are the kinds who have horror stories: the ones with dangerous boyfriends; the ones who bonked their husbands; the ones with such terrible personal problems that they left in tears; or, worst of all, the ones who are so perfect, so bonded, that life falls apart completely when they leave.

But just as worrying as about potentially nasty nanny is the fact that by bringing them in to your home to work there legally, they not only cost a shedload in tax and National Insurance, but they have full employment rights. Most of us are employees of a company, but that means that the company bears the cost of any issues which might – and do – come up with its employees. You may not think of yourself as a business when you hire someone to come and look after your children, but you should. Even if you can contemplate this very elite kind of childcare, the cost may be considerably higher than you tell yourself.

Then there is the nanny share. I have watched people walk unwittingly into a potentially hellish nanny share, only to realize later that there are almost always problems. The nanny usually has a stronger relationship with one family in particular, which creates split loyalties. Also, do you want your child in its own surroundings, or in someone else's home?

I would advise anyone thinking of getting into a nanny share to think through very clearly in advance what will happen if things don't work out, rather than focusing on the immediate need. All too often couples have to find a nanny quickly, and in desperation will take anyone they can find for their childcare cover.

 TOP TIP

Remember that if you have a nanny, you are an employer and are liable for their salaries in times of sickness, plus they have the full rights of employment law. Make sure you know what those rights are before you hire them.

Childminding has similar

pitfalls as regards sharing – by definition your childminder is qualified to look after more than one child at once in their home – but for some it can be the most flexible option. Sometimes it is better to send your precious tinys to several strangers at a nursery

TOP TIP

Try and build up a picture of what childcare is available long before you need it. Mix searching online and in local papers with word of mouth. But never get desperate and hire against your instinct.

rather than them just having one point of contact: the childminder. It can be tempting to look less hard at how they live and what kind of activities they will take your child to when you are not using their services more than a few hours a week. That said, we had a wonderful childminder, a mum at school, for our youngest. So much of good childcare falls to luck and timing, it is scarily unpredictable.

RECIPE

RECIPE:	TELEPHONE TEA
TIME:	Five or ten minutes, usually.
INGREDIENTS:	Email to organize, and of course a telephone to conduct the meeting with.

I know we all say 'We should get together' for work meetings, but if you're honest, how many meetings do you actually need to have in which you're in the same room? The late Anita Roddick, founder of the Body Shop, famously banned people from sitting down at meetings because it encouraged them to lurk about longer than they should. I go one further: limit your actual meetings and have 'Telephone Tea' instead. This is a delicious way to be more focused and saves time for all concerned. You can email agendas and issues to discuss, and forward-plan a time to actually have the meeting in a much quicker way. Obviously you have to use your judgement. If a person is going to be offended because you can't spare the time to meet in person, or you need to pore over some documents together, then don't have 'Telephone Tea' for its own sake, but when you do: enjoy!

7

The F-Word: Flexibility

Flexibility is the new Holy Grail in work–life balance. We all crave it, like toned thighs and winning the lottery. For most of us it is a theory, not a reality. As the Fawcett Society says: 'Employees across the UK have clear aspirations to work in jobs which enable them to combine work and family life. It is time for the government to acknowledge the weight of public opinion in favour of flexible working by showing leadership on this agenda.'

If we all had real flexibility at work it would look something like this:

- Paring down what we do to the essentials, and cutting out the excess of meetings, emails, unecessary networking and therefore lowering the actual amount of hours it takes to 'do' your job

---

- Figuring out how you can best work flexibly and proving it to your employer so they support rather than resist
- Being bold with ideas – acting less like an employee and more like a partner with the same goal as your boss
- Deciding with your whole team in which you play your part what would work best for the overall output of your company or organization, as well as you individually

In other words you would create a system which allows productivity and flexibility.

If this sounds like some kind of management-speak that's because it is. I'm a small business owner and to that extent I confess I'm somewhat torn on the topic of flexible working. I'm all in favour in principle, and I am a working mother who relies on it myself, but I recognize that despite flexible working being a noble aspiration, it is much harder to put into practice.

My old friend Rosie Boycott, founding feminist icon, caused uproar when she admitted that her small farm-holding business would be under threat if her thirty-something female employee became pregnant, which would mean Rosie had to find cover for her and hold her job open for many months. She had a point, and it's one that is difficult to raise in a culture that deals with rights in isolation, rather than looking at what is also practical and right for different kinds of businesses.

The law obliges all employers regardless of size to offer some kind of flexibility to employees, and in particular to parents with children under the age of six or, if disabled, eighteen. By 2010 maternity leave can be extended for a full year.

I'm no fan of asking government to stump up for everything, but I would like to see a distinction made between large organizations, which can absorb the loss of a member of staff through illness or parenthood (absence has the same impact, even if the cause is different), and small ones, which can't. I'd like to see a fund set up by a consortium of business

TOP TIP

Be organized without being too rigid. When you plan too much it just gets blown away by life's many suprises. Prepare to have to reconfigure things frequently.

players, similar to Boris Johnson's 'Mayor's Fund' in London where money is put into a pot for social projects, to allow small companies to offer flexible working. I'd also like a pot of money to be allocated through the Federation of Small Businesses, the CBI or the IoD to allow small-business owners to apply for financial help to aid working parents, as well as expertise on secondment if they need it.

CASE STUDY

Avril, a travelling beautician from Newcastle, is single with no children.

The reason that I start work late is because I choose to finish at 11ish in the evening. This flexibility in my life comes from not having to be home in the evenings to take care of another person. I do this four nights a week and people have on many occasions suggested that I need to see more clients during the day so that I needn't work in the evenings (as if it is not my choice to live like this but a necessity).

I do, however, like my bed too much in the morning. At midnight I'm often wide awake and active. I may have brought in washing, logged my takings in the ledger and am still doing emails. These are things that I would not want to do the morning as I intend lying about resting before work. I would not swap evening work for anything.

Bending the Rules

Legally, everyone in the UK is entitled to work flexibly, and yet the truth is that some jobs 'bend' better than others.

Deborah, forty-eight, from Mansfield, Nottingham, is a single mother with a ten-year-old daughter. She is also a full-time specialist nurse working in a health trust that has flexible working policies. But, as she explained to me, 'What works on paper isn't what works in practice. When it comes to the crunch you let people down – or people feel let down – if you leave early and there is no one to cover for you because no one is doing your job or that bit of the job that needs doing when you walk out of the door. So the staff left behind get stressed and irritable.'

Flexible working suits Deborah because she can go home to her child early one day a week, but she is right: someone else has to cover for her. This needs to be worked out and agreed, but all too often only the issue of 'rights' is addressed while the question of cover is ignored.

CASE STUDY

Sally, forty-two, a housing association officer, has two children and lives with her partner Simeon, a carpenter.

I had a job share at my previous job, which should have worked brilliantly because we were two mothers of similar age with similar work experience. But what actually happened was that she left everything to me and so I had to cram a week's worth into two and a half days.

The arrangement was meant to allow me to be with the kids but on the days when I was with them I was exhausted right from the

> beginning of the week. Although the job share could have worked, we should have had some sort of trial period first, because it ended up being the toughest year of my life. The terrible unfairness of it only added to the workload.
>
> In the end I complained about her, which just made the situation even worse, so I did what most women do when they feel they are being badly treated at work, which is just move to another job.

Something is wrong with flexible working in Britain, because we have one of the lowest take-up rates in Europe – some 50 per cent compared to over 90 per cent in Germany for instance – and yet in some jobs working flexibly clearly impacts badly, either on co-workers or on consumers.

In the City, no amount of flexible working laws will change the culture: once you begin to leave early to rush to get back to your nanny, or nursery, or even, shock horror, your child in order to put them to bed, you lose status and get passed over for promotion. This was normal even before the City faced financial ruin making additional pressure on all those lucky enough to still be employed there. On the other hand, in some jobs, such as the public sector, the culture may be flexible in theory, but in practice the mood sours if childless staff feel unduly disadvantaged. Flexible working needs to work for everyone, not just people with children. Not as another law – God knows employers have enough of these to comply with – but as a culture change.

 TOP TIP

Design flexible working with your boss which means you can be every bit as productive without being stuck in the office. Ask for it regardless of whether you have children or not. Agree a review period.

If you can do your job on a flexible basis that is agreed both with your boss and within your organization, then great, but flexible time itself needs to be negotiable. Some jobs simply aren't so flexible. If you work on a farm and want to go home just before milking time, is the farmer going to postpone the milking just to suit you? Or if you are a GP and want to take a day off every Wednesday, how happy will your patients be when their access to you is cut by a fifth?

I do know a woman who gave up a very high-flying career in the City because she just couldn't cope with the macho culture. She was demotivated by the attitudes of her colleagues following her pregnancies, because they understood only one gear at work: full throttle. She left her job and never looked back, but she had a big cushion: working in the City, she had built up enough of a nest egg to pay off her mortgage in full before she was thirty-five years old. Another ex City worker I know has gone 'Portfolio' with a number of executive roles instead of a full-time job. She much prefers it because although there are some 'down times' when she is not as busy as she would like, she feels so much more free than she did before.

The Devil is in the Detail

I think we confuse a number of things when we talk about flexible working. For a start, it is not the same as part-time working, or shift working, or staggered working. If you work your quota of hours, but for some of them you're on the top of a mountain and for others you're at the computer at home, or you stop-and-start to fit around childcare, that's flexible working. If you try to cram in an extra fifteen hours of work in a week when you aren't supposed to be doing any extra hours because technically you are down to working for only three days, that's overtime. And if you really work from a mountain top, that is remote working, which

TOP TIP

If you can, go freelance, but don't be made to feel that you are doing less of a job just because you are working from home.

means more time for Telephone Tea but not enough for the meetings you might actually need to have face to face.

Real flexibility – like the devil – is in the detail. It means different things, large and small. Do you have privacy in your office so that you can telephone your bank or school or doctor (or lover) as needs be? Do you have a meeting schedule that you control enough to be able to tack an errand on to either side of it? Or do you simply have the right kind of employer who understands and who also offers the kind of work that allows you to 'self-manage' on a sensible basis, rather than having to request time off, and gives you the flexibility to take care of the small, daily stuff that can't be done after 5 p.m. or be left until the weekend?

CASE STUDY

Anna, thirty-two, a civil engineer, has one son aged six. She is married to John, a personal trainer.

I don't talk about my son much at work. I am the only female in the office and as the men talk very little about their children when they are together I feel very uncomfortable about doing it myself. My husband takes the kids to school and picks them up again, so my children have no effect on my hours.

In such a male environment I am definitely suppressing part of myself, but I know I would never get promotion if I let slip that I had been up all night tending a sick child, or if I was overheard talking to my husband about a play date for my son or something that happened at his school. I go to the toilet to ring him instead.

It's pathetic really but when I wanted to go to my son's Christmas play I pretended that I had a terrible headache with a slight hint that it might have had something to do with a Christmas party I went to the night before. That was more accept-able than going to see my son being the king in the nativity play. How mad is that!

And how much does flexibility feel like a perk or a specific culture rather than a necessity? Does the right to work flexibly – whether enshrined by law or company policy or just born of common consent and common sense – mean you save on childcare, or have time to keep fit, or just feel in control?

I envy the office space of a friend, complete with its snazzy bar, newspaper reading area, and extraordinary modern furniture and lights, all of which was designed for a staff of several hundred. This office space says 'flexible' in a laid-back, cool way. It conveys to staff, 'You can decide when to take a break, or have a think, or have a meeting, you don't have to be hunched over your desk.' I have no idea what their actual work–life policy is, but I know that they provide a working

 TOP TIP

It's never all right to miss your child's big events. Get there by hook or by crook because, if you don't, they'll always remember that you weren't there.

atmosphere that suggests that, underneath the gloss, it is a good place to work as well. This is clever because of course employers would like their staff to be visible to them quite a lot of the

TOP TIP

Be aware of your employer's needs, not just your own. Make up any 'undertime' with 'overtime'.

time – it creates a sense of security. And if you have an ultra-nice office, people will want to work there.

Another benefit of working in an office is the company they provide. There is nothing to beat a culture of camaraderie and shared mission, even though the drawbacks can outweigh the benefits. I do think the risk of everything from bitchy office politics to timewasting on emails to people sitting next to you are some of the perils which can be reduced by having a flexible working policy.

CASE STUDY

Jenny, a TV executive, has two children.

Be very clear with your colleagues about your working practices from the outset and be determined to make it work. Don't talk about your children and your home responsibilities with senior colleagues unless you can do so positively and without mentioning the difficulties of having two lives. Keep telling yourself not to feel guilt because it is a useless emotion that only makes it worse.

Three-Way Streets

I work pretty flexibly. I have designed exactly how I work because, for me, flexibility is in my top three priorities for working conditions. These are:

1. Loving what I do, always being interested in and energized by my work.
2. Earning enough to provide for my family, rainy days, and gel nails.
3. Being flexible in order to share childcare and have a good quality of life.

As an employer, I also have three concerns about flexible working – including my own:

1. Ensuring that the business operates smoothly and successfully without hiccups.
2. Giving employees enjoyable work to do with variety and flexibility built in.
3. Having contingencies in place to cover illness, time off, and maternity/paternity leave.

Of course all these priorities and concerns go together. If you feel you enjoy your work, the chances are that your workplace enjoys you. And if your employer or senior colleagues feel you 'get' the job and do it well, they will bend over backwards to make flexibility work where possible. But it has to work three ways too: for you, for your employer, and for the customer or client that your employer provides for.

Your flexibility only feels good if it doesn't bend the comfort zone of others out of shape. There are some times when I'm flexible *backwards*: I work late, I start early, I miss the school run. My working life is not a uniform production line; it is not rigid, so I can't be. And neither is my home life. So when one of the children is going through a phase of being

☞ TOP TIP

Work odd hours rather than conformist hours if you can, so that early shifts or late shifts when the kids need you are free.

unhappy or needy, or Alaric's bad knee gives out and he has to have early-morning physiotherapy, or when the pace at work ebbs rather than flows, I also tilt the balance the other way and flex *forwards* to the family.

CASE STUDY

Polly, forty-four, is a service manager for a charity, and has three teenage children. She has been with her Italian partner, Marco, for twenty-one years.

I have stayed in my current job for over ten years, apart from a brief period where I worked somewhere else. Perhaps because it is a charity for children, my employers are very flexible if I have to leave early to pick up the kids. Once when all three children had whooping cough they were really understanding. The flexibility goes both ways though. I will always try to make up any time that I have had to take off, or work late the following evening if I have had an emergency. If your employer is flexible over your family, it makes you much more conscientious, more likely to stay and give the job your best.

I always make sure I have Fridays off, and this works brilliantly for me. My job is the kind of thing you have to leave behind once you get home, otherwise it would be extremely stressful, and I am quite strict about that. This means I have three days of family and friends. Then I go into work on a Monday relaxed and feeling as if I am on top of the family stuff. It helps level things out.

My previous job seemed totally inflexible. The stress of having a family and employers who expect you to work late and prove yourself was just too much. I was unhappy and so were my family. I don't see why you should have to pretend that you don't have children.

Crop Rotation

The more I think about work in relation to the rest of life, the more I realize that the only way off the See-Saw is to think about prioritizing areas of your life in rotation, not all at once. So, for a few months you may have to work super-hard, in the way teenagers do in exam season. Then you take your foot off the pedal just enough to refocus on what has lain fallow: is it your fitness, or your family, or your emotional life? The demand to do well in each aspect of our lives is so great now that we will simply burn out if we do too much. All it took for me to get dangerously ill one year was a toxic combination of not working efficiently, having too much to do, and having a crisis over childcare.

I know now that I could have done some forward planning and probably avoided getting ill at all. I could have looked ahead six months, thought about what was coming up, and allowed some time to work out where the overload was likely to come from. Big events both at work and at home can conspire to wear you out. Moving house and divorce are known culprits, but what about the smaller stuff: a marital bad patch, a business growth spurt, children being bullied and needing extra time from you?

Flexibility needs to begin in our heads, as we work out what we need and when we need it. Only then can we figure out what the obstacles are, and whether the finger of blame points only to 'them', the people who run the country or pay our wages, or to 'us', who run our own lives.

On the See-Saw: Amanda

Amanda runs F1 Recruitment. She has two sons, aged eleven and twelve, from a previous marriage. Two years ago she married a widowed teacher with two adult children.

My aim is to able to fulfil my potential as a professional, which means achieving my personal career goals whilst also being a supportive, loving and involved wife, a mother and a stepmother, a sister and a daughter, as well as being godmother to ten children and aunt to three nephews and nieces. Keeping healthy is essential to achieving all this. Getting the work–life balance right will also enable my husband and me to travel, and to integrate other non-earning opportunities into our lives in the longer term.

Yes, I do believe work–life balance is achievable, although it requires strength of mind, relentless energy, and focused application, especially in the area of time management.

Work–life balance is exactly that – a balancing act. In any one day, week or month, the balance can get out of kilter. It is important to have enough self-awareness to realize when the balance is wrong and a partner who can help you understand how to correct the balance if work is dominating.

As they grow older, children understand the pressures on a working mother and learn that they can help this balancing act with little contributions (such as keeping their rooms tidy, clearing the table after meals, managing their homework or their revision timetable). Teamwork is essential within a family to achieve work–life balance. In a team everyone has to contribute but everyone also has to have their say. It is important that all members of the family are able to give feedback openly in an informal way. We always talk about teamwork at home.

Career and Flexible Working

In your twenties choose a profession that you think you will enjoy that also lends itself to a female career, and stick to it. Become an expert in your chosen field. Choose a company or an industry with care, one that actively promotes female promotion in the workforce and offers flexible working or career breaks.

If you work from home, have a designated room that your family know is your space. And discipline yourself to work in chunks of time – have work time and family time. Don't muddle the two up.

Childcare

My boys went to nursery, which worked well for us, and then we had a nanny pick them up from school once they were of school age. I have always been home by 6.30 p.m. and have always been there for story time/bedtime. I think this is a really important time of the day. Children like routine and the security of knowing Mum is home!

I have always done 70 per cent of the school pick-ups and drop-offs. On three days a week I leave my children at school at 8 a.m. and catch the 8.13 a.m. train to get me into the office in London at 9.15. The other days I work from home, when again I drop them off and collect them from school. Granny picks them up one day a week, which the boys love, and my husband picks them up on the two other days.

I was a single mum from when my boys were two and one until they were eight and seven, when continuity and security were even more important for them. I have since remarried and have inherited two stepchildren (now twenty-four and twenty-one), who both add another dimension to our busy lives. At weekends when they are all home (with their other halves) the house is a hive of activity – it's wonderful.

Relationships

My boys have quality time with all of us. Car journeys of ten minutes or more are great times to chat. I say goodnight to my boys every night and we always have ten minutes or so reading or just chatting about the day's activities. We walk as a family and we do things together at the weekend. The boys also spend quality time with their father, who lives in London, and they stay with him every other weekend. He spends Christmas with us and he comes to parents' meetings with my husband and me.

I have a great husband who is my soulmate. We have been together for four years now and got married two years ago. His wife died of cancer after they had been married for twenty-five happy years.

My first husband left me when my boys were just one and two years old. I went through a very nasty divorce and had six hard years on my own. My second husband and I have glued our two families together and, two years on, the six of us have settled in well. He and I discuss everything. When you run your own business it is important to be able to get things off your chest. He is a teacher, and used to be on the senior management team at a leading public school, so he understands the stresses of being in a leadership role where the buck stops with you. He has a high emotional intelligence and is a great listener. I hope I provide him with the same skills.

Well-Being

Because I work from home two days a week, I swim a mile a week on one morning after the school drop-off and play a vigorous game of singles tennis on the other morning. I also walk to and from Charing Cross station to our offices in Oxford Street on the three days I am in London, which is about 2.2 miles a day.

My husband and I also manage to get away once every seven weeks for a long weekend where we walk – seven or eight miles at a time – or cycle. We both find we work in six or seven intense weekly chunks (I guess the school calendar helps this). We are ruthless about booking our breaks and we really look forward to them.

As soon as we return from our long summer holiday each year (three weeks), we book the next one. We have a week on our own first, just the two of us, and then the family and extended family (currently there are fourteen of them) join us at a villa – this year in Sicily.

Organization and Prioritizing

Whenever the juggle feels overwhelming I work through my To Do List and then take a day off to get things back into perspective. To get rid of stress I exercise, which usually does the trick, although sharing the stress and asking for help play their part too.

I have a home To Do List and a diary, and a work To Do List, which I update religiously every evening before I go to bed. I sleep incredibly well for seven hours minimum every night. Every weekend I have a lie-in with my trade mags and the weekend newspapers. Writing things down helps me enormously. I was lucky to have been trained very early in my career in time management and desk management. I am getting better at asking for help.

Work–Life Balance

If you asked me my single biggest tip for having work–life balance, I would say: have a great supportive husband who is ten years older than you, respects you enormously, is a great cook, and loves shopping. In return, you must keep your end of the bargain and ensure he has clean socks in his drawers and that his ties are dry-cleaned regularly.

Remember to laugh and have fun. Be able to laugh at yourself when you are being ridiculous. We laugh a lot in our house. We always eat together as a family in the evenings and Sunday roasts are a key time of the week. We also like to rip the cork out of a bottle, play bumper games of Monopoly, and indulge in our favourite family participation game: 'What would be your favourite song on your desert island?' The iPod gets a lot of use!

IF I DON'T HAVE TIME TO WALK **TO** WORK, I WALK **AT** WORK.

8

Fitness Freaking Out

There are a couple of ways to look at the whole fitness thing. One is as a notch on your To Do List belt; the other is to realize that being fit is one of the most effective ways to keep you balanced on the See-Saw.

I have lots of natural energy and limit my daily intake of coffee to three espressos washed down with lots of water. However, the idea of exercise fills me with dull dread. I was not a hockey girl, nor a tennis girl, and definitely not a skiing girl. I love swimming but only for the first ten minutes, after which a sort of rigor mortis of boredom kicks in.

So, all in all, I have long been freaking out about the increased pressure to Feel the Burn and Get Fit. I have been in a boxing ring with the biscuit tin for many years, and naturally if you are a bit podgy and stodgy the last thing you feel like doing is parading a less-than-ideal body around a gym.

Jenny, fifty, runs her own catering company. She has one child aged eighteen and lives with her partner Simon, an occupational therapist.

I think that everyone has bits of themselves that they are horrified by and mine are my arms. I felt that from one year to the next they turned into what they call 'Miami arms' – great dimpled hunks of meat that wobbled if I lifted them.

I had tried the gym when I was younger and loathed it – the smell, the vanity, and the lonely grind of it – and I know myself pretty well by now. I almost have to trick myself into exercise. So I just put dumb-bells by the telly and every time I wanted to watch something I would do some weights. They got a bit heavier too as I got stronger. Because I was pretty rigid about doing it and didn't even care that Simon found it 'unrelaxing', my arms do look a lot better. I think I can even wear sleeveless things now without frightening the horses.

Getting off the Yo-Yo and on to the See-Saw

Britain started to become a nation of fatties at the point when we all began to have to work such long hours that there was no time to keep fit and all those obese-making ready meals were just too readily available.

Fast food has always been marketed as time saving, although cooking real food is almost as fast as any other kind of cooking. The companies that manufacture ready meals have hit on a winning formula to serve up comfort food to people who are time-poor, stressed, and overworked, who mean to get fit but, er, never quite find the time, and who feel too sludgy by and large to make the effort.

Part of the fitness problem is, of course, that it feeds into the fantasy of perfection. I absolutely hate the phrase 'No pain, no gain' because to teenage boys and girls 'gain' means a washboard stomach (a particularly remote ideal after three pregnancies) and

TOP TIP

Regard fitness as being about increasing production, not vanity. Better to have lasting energy, anytime.

God knows how many 'ab crunches' to achieve it.

CASE STUDY

David, forty-four, a film lecturer, is married to Jane and has two children aged twelve and fourteen.

I realized I had become one of those men that I used to laugh at when I was a teenager – who look as if they have got a football stuck down their jumper. I was all stomach. When I got naked I was shocked at myself because I looked like a huge toddler.

When I turned forty I was absolutely determined to do something about it. I went on a gruelling diet and ignored my wife's silent disapproval of 'yet another faddy diet'. I also went running and joined a gym. I lost four stone, which felt absolutely amazing. I really did feel reborn.

However, as everyone said, the difficulty after the initial elation is that reality sets in and it is not the complete transformation that you expect. The truth is that you are exactly the same person as you were before, only thinner, which comes as something of a revelation. I thought that everything would be different but of course it isn't. All the same, I did keep most of the weight off and it has become less of an effort to maintain it because I have now retrained myself.

While the rest of us muddle along, only a very diehard bunch make time for the gym in a meaningful way and get that special feeling they call an 'endorphin rush', which, frankly, sounds a bit like the orgasm scene in *When Harry Met Sally*.

So how do we achieve fitness – all that yummy toning and tightening and energy and smugness – without using up all our available time in the process? Well, remember that this isn't a book of answers but a book of ideas-come-recipes, which may or may not make your life tasty and wholesome... Here is what worked for me.

Idiot-Proof Atkins

I have been a yo-yo eater for years without actually dieting. Like the author and columnist India Knight, whose book *The Idiot-Proof Diet* made a big impact on me, I thought diets were for ninnies, although unlike her I did feel a tremendous anxiety about size and scoffing (she just noticed she was getting huge and decided to do something about it).

The Atkins Diet is coming back in fashion with a modern twist to include more fruit and veg in an otherwise protein-heavy set of meals. This suits me, because no amount of coffee alone can help me reach the energy levels I really need. For me the ideal combination is low carbs or no carbs, not just because it makes weight control actually attainable, but because the energy pay-off is so noticeable. By changing the way I ate, I gave myself extra energy, therefore extra productiveness. As a result I guess I actually gained something like an hour, or even two, each day when I'd otherwise be pretty sluggish.

Having apparently got to the

 TOP TIP

Dump a carbohydrate-based diet in favour of a Mediterranean one, based on fish, nuts, cheese, fruit and veg.

right size and shape at last without the aid of a starvation diet or a gastric band, I needed to think about the exercise bit.

 **TOP TIP**

Combine exercise with a green way of getting to the office: put your trainers in a bag, get off a stop early on the tube, and walk.

Whilst I struggle with work–life balance, I have zero physical balance. I wobble on bicycles and fall down skating. An ex-boyfriend once cruelly joked that my dancing was 'trotting on the spot', which was, sadly, an accurate observation. As for dance or exercise classes, the whole teeth-gnashing, competitive look is a no-no for me.

Pilates, yes, amazing and lovely but... too time-consuming. Too... sensible, although I do have some pilates DVDs, which gather dust along with the yoga DVDs and the yoga mat that my daughter Anoushka now uses for her terrifying somersaults.

But finally I found something that I enjoy and that works for me. Nothing racy like salsa or running, just plain old walking, I'm afraid. However, suddenly I Get It. I get the point of fitness. I can feel my body start to silt up if I have not done any exercise for a day, and I can feel my whole digestion and energy shift for the better when I have walked briskly for half an hour or longer.

The one practical drawback is that I end up lugging my trainers around in a bag, together with my papers and a change of heels, which can make it quite heavy. But as I'm something of a Bag Lady and collect nice big bags (and carrying my shoes in any kind of ugly holdall is out, as far as I'm concerned), I have just made it a wardrobe accessory thing.

RECIPE

RECIPE: TRAINERS-IN-A-BAG

TIME: Ideally forty-five minutes a day.

INGREDIENTS: A range of nice shoulder bags, trainers, socks, an iPod or MP3 player, and a daily destination

Around the time I decided that inching towards forty-five in terms of extra pounds as well as age wasn't a great idea, I faced the reality that I simply did not have time to go to the gym as often as it would take (plus, like you, I think there is only so much awful thumping music a grown girl can take), so I took up walking instead. What a revelation! The only thing I mind about this is that it means I have to walk around in ungainly trainers, which is not ideal, and the bag can be a bit heavy. But other than that, the rewards are great because walking is lovely, especially if you are listening to free podcast downloads or not-free-but-lovely music, and because it feels productive. You always finish up somewhere, usually at work, and, of course, although I admit this is not my first priority, it is also a green thing to do.

9

Me-Time (and the Non-Book Book Group)

The idea of me-time gets quite a good press on the See-Saw. We know what it means, for a start. We generally know we need it, and even deserve it, but getting it is another matter. Why is it important? There are three big reasons:

1. If you look after yourself, you can look after others better.
2. Recharging your batteries can make you see things afresh.
3. Why should me-time *not* be important? The alternative is to succumb to guilt (a bad idea).

What are the top routes to me-time? Well, the first is electing to have it at all. Daily. Yes, I said daily, not weekly, monthly or annually. Planning is everything, particularly as me-time can easily get halved or even abandoned in a dose of guilt (see the next chapter). You have to look at your day as well as your whole way of life and decide what you can afford in terms of time and money.

Of course, some me-time lends itself very well to spending money, but one advantage of the credit crunch is that it forces more meaningful ways to spend time. Sometimes I think I'm going to enjoy browsing in the shops till I drop but then I find that there is nothing worse than lugging great piles of clothes through to the changing room, or I get that overwhelmed, ugly-in-everything feeling. Finally it dawns on me at times like this that I probably need a good cry or a good gossip instead of a new jacket.

Me-time doesn't have to be a whole day at the spa. I'm the most impatient person on the planet and always struggled with yoga, even though I couldn't deny I felt very mellow afterwards. Then a wonderful yoga teacher called Anna Bluman spoke words that were music to my ears when she said that even five minutes a day would make a difference. Suddenly the pressure to have time to myself that I felt I didn't actually possess fell away, and I started to look at all sorts of possibilities for grabbing some quality time with myself that wouldn't take up hours and hours.

Gardening is great for this. I'm a total late bloomer regarding gardens. I used to be indifferent to them and was destined to kill any plant I came into contact with. Suddenly, as if it came with the grey hairs that began to cheekily populate my head, I found myself positively besotted with plants. I cheat, of course, by buying them ready-grown and then I just put them in pots and water them, but even ten minutes a day of this makes me very much calmer, with significantly less chance of bellowing at some small person (also grown by me).

The Non-Book Book Group

One of the great images of a woman having me-time is of her cradling a phone against her ear, yakking. As a toddler Roman would grab a plastic toy telephone, put it up against his ear, and shout, 'Uh-huh, uh-huh, yes, I'm on the phone.'

I must say that phoning someone I adore talking to has to be in my top ten me-time activities. My friend Ruth and I can talk for a good hour before either of us has the remotest inclination to shut up. We talk about her adult children and my brood, our work, our men, our brothers, our clothes, and our houses, after which we move on to state-of-the-nation topics and back again.

I joined a book group to try to extend the benefits of girly discussion but I found I hated it. All that homework – reading a book that had been chosen at random rather than on personal recommendation – and in any case after making the effort to read it most of the group would disintegrate into gossiping within about ten minutes. So I broke away and started something much better: the Non-Book Book Group. Same principle – gather some girlfriends together – but a different prop. Instead of books, they bring clothes and handbags to swap. And food. And talk of their lives and loves and hopes and fears.

In fact the idea for this book first came out of one of my non-book book group meetings. I asked everyone around the table to talk about what was on their minds. Some were coy and cautious. One said, 'Rubbish bin collections.' Then another blurted out, 'How to have good sex after fifteen years of marriage.' And suddenly the energy around the room was great. Not everyone over-shared, but everyone said something. I noticed that even my most stressed friend, who is coping with a special needs child with great stoicism, began to relax just a little.

The non-book book group had become like group therapy with great friends.

Polly, forty-four, is a service manager for a charity and has three teenage children. She has been with her Italian partner, Marco, for twenty-one years.

My female friends are very important to me. I have a group of very old friends and we regularly see each other, cook meals for each other, go for walks, go to the cinema, or go out to eat. Some of them have children and families, and some of them don't, which is good because it means that the conversation is not always about children and men.

We are all quite different and usually have a laugh. It is very relaxing and provides instant relief from family and work life. My partner Marco has a lot of interests and a wide circle of male friends, so we are both quite independent about having our own social life. This seems to work really well for us. I have just started a women's poker club, which is completely hilarious. Marco helps me run it, so we can do things together.

I go away with my circle of friends for weekends once or twice a year. At first I felt really anxious and really couldn't enjoy these trips because I hadn't been away from the children for any length of time. It was really hard. On more than one occasion I thought I was about to have a panic attack. However, I have carried on making myself have these breaks because I think they are a good thing to do.

A couple of months later one of my oldest friends came to London for her father's funeral. Five of us who have known each other for more than thirty years sat around just as if we were in a novel, drinking wine and eating chicken and greens in ginger and soy, followed by oodles of ice cream. When the wine ran out Jane, my grieving friend, found some (frankly revolting) plum brandy in a cupboard. We all had a tipple of this and talked and giggled until the small hours.

 TOP TIP

I defy you not to enjoy *Mama Mia* the movie. Find a film or show you can go to with friends and just *enjoy* the escapism.

Of course the whole point of the non-book book group is not to have work to do (having a book you have to read rather than want to read is kind of work and, anyway, the efficiency worker bee in me just thinks you should send a link to a book you recommend and have done with it) but rather to see your friends and make friends with your friends' friends. In short, whatever your excuse, that's fine, but get talking, sharing, and, of course, finish off the plum brandy.

 TOP TIP

Make time, even once a week, to get out of the house and do something energetic and fun. Don't think that emailing on Facebook equates to a social life: it doesn't.

Dinner Ladies and Gents

I know it is a good problem to have, but my husband does all the cooking. So whilst I don't prepare breakfast, lunch, tea or supper out of necessity, if I'm not careful I miss out on doing something I like very much. Between us both we have collected a seriously large range of cookery books. My heroes are the Ottolenghi duo and Nigel Slater, while my American friend Nina Planck is a wonderful food writer specializing in what she calls Real Food. So I have the recipes, I just have to invent reasons to cook.

Having dinner parties has become a way of getting a social life without having to be out in the evenings, We probably have people over for supper every six weeks or so, plus a weekend lunch for families and kids about once a month.

> **☞ TOP TIP**
>
> Form your own non-book book group and decide who you want in it. Make it a project and then ask everyone to bring a friend and rotate the organizing

If you spend a lot of time rushing about, getting to and from an office, and dealing with schools, nannies, or nurseries – on the phone, on the computer, and on the go – slowing down can be much the hardest thing you do.

CASE STUDY

Smarayda, thirty-eight and single, is a freelance writer and sub-editor.

When I first started freelancing I was taking block bookings and writing in the evenings, saying yes to everything and not taking holidays. I wore myself down, and was looking and feeling shattered.

I knew I had to do something about it because all I was doing was working and I really wasn't enjoying it. I didn't have anyone to tell me to ease off and so I tended to spend all my time working and earning as much money as I could. I became greedy and didn't realize that I was missing out on life.

I decided to do something about how awful I was feeling, so I started to plan properly, looking ahead at the year and being much more organized about blocking in work, but also blocking in holidays. I would take on work with the condition that I had a two-week break in the middle of it. I became much more assertive and seemed to get much more respect as a result. I also started taking on project work that I could do at home so that I could manage my own time.

I make sure now that every real blitz of work always has a lovely break at the end of it. I also like treats and arrange in advance things like tickets for the theatre or live music, so that I always have something pleasurable to look forward to, which is particularly important when working from home.

I also have to be really disciplined about not letting friends drop round in the middle of the day and make clear to them that just because I work from home doesn't mean that I am up for a chat and a coffee.

I now have much more of a balanced life but it took me getting extremely run down to take stock.

I think finding something you can slow down to do, and enjoy doing, is essential to getting your See-Saw down from the adrenalin high or up from the doldrums of routine. As I mentioned, this is preparing food for a dinner party, precisely because I don't do the daily cooking and because the sight of our kitchen doesn't make me think of chores like washing up. (I have long since been banned by Alaric from loading the dishwasher on some weird masculine pretext that I don't stack it correctly but, hey, I'm not complaining.)

So picture me in the kitchen. The children are in bed or off in their rooms, the computer is off, the man is watching *Taggart*, and the iPod is on. I'm listening to some folk or some classical guitar, and I have a very mellow, wafty candle on the go as I float cheerily about, humming and doing things that make me feel like a real cook, so that after an hour of this I have slowed up and calmed down from all the rushing and daily adrenalin.

TV Suppers and Facebook Friends

I'm more of a news junkie TV-wise, but every now and then a show comes along that becomes my friend. For about nine months I got into *EastEnders* and became hooked. At the time I was finding it really hard to unwind when I got home from work. I constantly wanted to keep looking at emails and felt beached in between work and home modes. The absorbing, utterly over-the-top plotlines and characters were great to dive into, especially as all the i-Player technology had just arrived to let me play things back when it suited.

I also have to admit – as my online friends know all too well – that I have a reasonably advanced Facebook habit. I do not endlessly roam around the internet communicating on things like Twitter, but I was hooked the minute I saw Facebook, in the way people were with

Friends Reunited at the beginning. I would say I spend a good ten minutes a day updating my profile, and sending and replying to a couple of messages. Every now and then I fill in some details about my life.

Alaric always makes me laugh as he seems to know whenever I'm on Facebook and starts to hover behind me, singing, 'Facebook, Facebook, I'm a sad person with nothing to do but go on Facebook,' but I don't care. The perfect me-time is often something your other half can't understand at all.

TOP TIP

Take your laptop to bed. Download your favourite TV programme and watch it balanced on your knees. It is not only very decadent but allows you to actually watch something without being interrupted.

CASE STUDY

Liz, forty-four and divorced, is a freelance film-maker.

My recipe for success is the daily Buddhist practice that I've been doing for seventeen years now. I am convinced that this sacrosanct discipline – when I clear my mind of all tasks and chatter, to access a calm and clear wisdom within – has helped me to create my life as it is now and got me through the times that seemed impossible.

My life is probably quite different to that of most women of my age in that I'm divorced, childfree, a freelance film-maker, and in a very fulfilling, relatively new relationship of two years where we each live in our own homes, three and a half hours apart. To many women, it will appear gloriously clutter-free.

For me the biggest issue has been dealing with the lack of structure and isolation in my life. Being freelance means that I don't have a ready-made office network, creating social interaction around me. Being childfree means I have no concept of when half-term falls or the logistics of school runs, which not only leaves me out of sync with my peers but also removes a huge piece of social infrastructure.

Freelance life can be feast or famine, and film-making can be arduous and all consuming. No sooner is one job finished than I am already looking out for the next one. Taking a holiday is a risk, not a luxury.

The imbalance in my life clanged home a couple of years ago. I had just finished a very intensive, eighteen-month, unusually lucrative film-making contract with a global investment bank. I came home and my phone didn't ring for a week.

I realized that things had to change. I fessed up my situation to my friends – who all thought I was having a gloriously sociable time when in fact I was often miserable – and asked for their support.

Instead of fearing being unemployed, I learned to see myself as being 'time rich' between jobs. I started to use that time to do things that nourished me but felt rather indulgent, like painting or reading up on technical editing notes or spending quality time with my busy friends in London.

Life feels more balanced now than it ever has.

Because I'm Worth It

If you gave me a year's worth of tanning salon vouchers, I'd throw them away. Ditto for facials, which I hate with a passion. But body beauty treatments? Another matter entirely.

I found a brilliant accupuncturist, on recommendation: my favourite way to find new people or services. I was recovering from pneumonia and kept getting chest infections. Within a couple of months of acupuncture treatment the infections had stopped, but I also realized that I came out of the salon positively floating with good energy and calmness.

TOP TIP

Go for a walk without your mobile. Remember that our parents were not contactable every second and we survived. There is nothing so terrible about a delay in replying to a call or email. It is rare to miss a true emergency but we behave as if one is constantly around the corner.

So for me, me-time is also beauty time, which is also health time.

Empty Time

On the rare occasions that I take time off outside of the school holidays, I can potter about the house or wander outside on nearby Hampstead Heath or in Highgate Woods. On these days I try to plan to do nothing. It is easier said than done. I automatically think I will nip to Ikea, or go to the gym, or visit my friend who has had a stroke, or visit my dad who is in his nineties, or... I plan and plot and before I know it I've done something. But every now and then I don't succumb, and I just drift without any plans at all, which feels so delicious it is almost indecent.

TOP TIP

So what do you have to do to discover what you really enjoy and what calms you? Is it something active or passive? Something you need a day for or an hour? Everyone varies but everyone has something. Find out what yours is.

Sleep is also the perfect me-time. Sleep and good duvets, crisp cotton sheets, a tidy and clutter-free room. Daytime naps are great but here's the secret: don't snooze on a full stomach, or you may wake up more grumpy and tired than when you went to lie down.

I fully intend to install a snooze room at the office one of these days so everyone can get a little time to themselves, even before they officially clock off.

Them-Time

I haven't talked much about caring for children with special needs, or elderly relatives, both of which tend to take up every ounce of time and energy there is going. Although I have had no direct experience of this, I know from observing both friends and family members who have nursed ill people that it can be all consuming.

Is it even possible to think about the niceties of 'being good to

yourself' in these circumstances?
Obviously not, or not much.
When you are in crisis, driving up
and down the motorway as my
friend Rachel did every day for

TOP TIP

Always make some time for others, a friend or neighbour in need.

weeks before her father died, or like Else, caring for her elderly, incontinent father while holding down a day job and returning to be his night nurse, it took its toll.

The me-time I'm talking about will obviously work best when your life is on some kind of even keel. If you know that the See-Saw is lurching downwards with the weight of all your stress and overload, you need to tune back in with yourself. Me-time as such shouldn't be an indulgence; it has quite a serious function to restore and rebalance. Me-time makes you enjoy life more but also work more effectively. So don't feel a cissy about it; think of it as productivity *enhancement.*

CASE STUDY

Franc, forty-eight, is a chef with three children aged six, seven and ten. He lives in London with his wife Gill.

When I tell my friends that I live with my mother-in-law, they usually groan and commiserate with me. Actually I adore my mother-in-law.

When she was diagnosed with Parkinson's disease, she invited all of us to come and live in her house because it was so much bigger than ours, and we divided it up as much for her privacy as our own. I find her a very entertaining, lovely person who has made our family life so much better. She wants to spend time alone with our kids and so we get more breaks alone together than anyone I know. As a result our relationship is in much better shape than those of many of our friends, who are knackered and don't have enough sex.

My wife finds it much more testing living with her mother than I do. I realize that her Parkinson's will set in and then she will need much more care from us, but we will both share it. I feel it is only right after all she has given us.

On the See-Saw: Sarah

Sarah, a writer, has no children and is on a See-Saw with MS.

Being a perfect parent as well as having a brilliant career is unachievable, over-ambitious, and unrealistic. Having a good job and being a good enough parent is achievable.

On Childless Women

In some jobs, such as journalism, there are inflexible timetables. This means at major family times – Christmas, school summer holidays, or simply for a couple of extra hours at the end of the day – the childless person will feel pressured to stay at work so that the parents can be at home. In my case, this was not a problem and I did not resent it. (I thought it was fair, and having a place where you are needed, free from the noise and hysteria of family-ness, can be enjoyable.)

But I have worked in offices where childless people did mind. They felt they were making several unrecognized sacrifices: first, by forgoing having children and a family life; second, by having their personal lives treated as nugatory – as of no worth; and third, by having their compensation for no children or family – which is free personal time – taken away from them for no reward or recognition.

I think mothers and childless women constitute almost separate tribes. I guess this causes painful feelings on both sides.

While the busy mother generally has a positive image or press, the childless spinster suggests such figures as the character played by Maggie Smith in A Room with a View *and suchlike – in other words, she is a figure of fun or pity, and, if she is attractive, of fear.*

On Disability and Illness

There are some similarities, as well as some differences, in the working needs of the mother and those of the not-well person. The not-well person's need for work with others – whether for the money, the community, the sense of value, or the stimulation – is just as great as that of a well person but it is obviously far harder to fulfil. Above a certain level of routine duties, it is extremely unlikely that a person with the reputation or stigma of illness will be given responsible work to do. (This may or may not be a 'glass ceiling', similar to the mother's difficulty.) However, the non-mother has the advantage, even if unwell, of being able to work outside fixed times.

There is, I think, a deep, unconscious fear of illness: that it will be contaminating, that the ill person (whatever the illness) is in some deep and absolute way a lesser person. I think attitudes are different towards mothers, who are in a transitory position. Whereas mothers have tots (charming little ones), disabled people are expected to have TOTs (Triumphs over Tragedy). Whereas the essence of motherhood is the need to be unselfish, the essence of illness can seem to be self-absorption and self-concern.

On Community

I think each of us is in a three-way relationship: work, family, community. I would say a true work–life balance should include the community at large. It is in the last area that childless people can take a foremost role. Many of our community organizations, volunteering systems, campaign groups, etc, are run by people without, at least young, children. They not only have the time and energy, they may (as in my case) positively seek the relationship with different generations that you might otherwise get only inside the family. I think these community organizations are the bedrock of a civilized society.

In my view modern society, with its complex and deep divisions of labour, is incompatible with being a whole person. This engenders guilt and resentment, phobias, forms of social autism, and also – see the *blogosphere – malice, spite, and* Schadenfreude. *In other words, unless there are community responses to the difficulties of combining the needs of work, family, and community life, too many people will be forced into finding unsatisfactory individual solutions. This works for the emotionally and physically healthy, but it can be a disaster for those with any frailty, leading to emotional and financial poverty, exclusion, loneliness, and various debilitating or dangerous psychological states.*

10

Guilt: The G-Spot You Can Always Find

Picture the scene. It is three o'clock in the morning. I hear a noise in my sleep and, in that odd moment of maternal intuition, leap out of bed to arrive on the landing just as one of our sons is violently sick everywhere. On the stairs, the walls, and everything in between. Once I have cleaned up said child, and installed him on the sofa with a bowl in front of him, I set about cleaning up and disinfecting the mess. Poor me, you say. Well, yes, but do you know what I'm really feeling and thinking? *Hooray*. Yes, hooray!

Not, you understand, because my pallid little boy is ailing – I'm reasonably sure it's a passing bug and of course he basically feels fine now that he has sicked up whatever it is – and not because I'm as fresh as a daisy, because I'm not; and certainly not because I'm any good whatsoever at household cleaning. In fact, I have to hunt very hard for everything because Alaric is the children's usual Sick

Monitor and generally oversees the cleaning of the house.

My hooray is this: it is a moment of pure Goodness. I can be a Good Mum, and a Good Hausfrau; I can be the kind of mother that I feel, deep down, at least some of the time, I should be. And in that moment, picking bits of sick off the carpet and wiping off the residue that has splattered lightly on every single picture hanging on the stairwell (wedding photo and all), I'm happy and fulfilled.

This is pathetic, but I'm happy that for once I feel no guilt. Guilt is always on trend and in season. Guilt is a hardy perennial. There is guilt because you have done something naughty and bad, which is also known as Remorse (think George Michael's 'Careless Whisper'). Then there is guilt as Lifestyle and Habit. A little bit of guilt is socially required in our society. You are expected to say that you feel awful because you haven't been able to sit down and help Freddie do his homework as you should; or because you splurged money even though the joint account is low; or because just by doing *too much* you have let people down, at work or at home.

It's pathetic because what kind of mother am I who generally leaves Dad to clean up the sick? (The first rule of guilt: seek it out wherever you can.) But it's also admirable or at least cloud-in-silver-lining-like, because in moments like this I realize that I am making quality time out of this middle-of-nowhere, dead-of-night time, which is, let's face it, better than nothing – on a week when maybe I have not once managed the school run, or have spent breakfast time yelling at the children to get their bags and *please* eat something.

I sit with my boy after the cleaning bonanza has finished, the two of us alone, tucked up under blankets, and we talk softly together until we both doze off and wake surrounded by suspi-

 TOP TIP

Try and laugh at the more ridiculous sides to guilt – rather that than cry.

cious, slightly envious other children, demanding, 'What are you doing? And what is that bucket... and smell?'

CASE STUDY

Adele, a teenage pregnancy co-ordinator for Wiltshire, has four sons aged between twenty-eight and nine. She lives with her Ghanaian husband, Harry.

I feel terrible guilt most of the time. It is a feeling I have learned to live with. I feel guilty for not being more with my kids, and guilty about my work, and guilty for not giving my husband the attention he deserves. He works very hard and is a great dad and I don't often have the time to let him know it. I don't think there is any answer to this.

We do try to go away on weekends together but probably not enough. When we do I'm always so amazed how well we get on. You don't realize how much your arguments are related to the children or your domestic duties. I think it's a good sign, when you are away together, if you actually like each other and talk to each other.

Finding the Spot

When I was becoming an adult there was much talk about the 'G-Spot'. It was one of those loony, quasi-medical claims that had women up and down the country rushing around with mirrors trying to examine themselves, not for empowerment but for clarity: can I *see* this mythical bit of me, which is supposed to exist so that we can all reach a state of sexual bliss by literally pushing a button?

Although the G-Spot idea was about women's sexual freedom, it really pushed the button of an F-word: Failure. Those likely to spend time doing things like working and juggling (more than snuggling) feel it most. This sense of failure created the *real* G-Spot, the one that we do find every time: GUILT.

My favourite Jewish joke is about the mother who gives her adult son two ties. Put one on, she urges. And he (being a Good Jewish Boy) obliges. The mother is enraged. 'What's the matter with the other one?' she demands. If you are a mother, or a daughter, or a person with responsibilities to other people, such as work colleagues, it is fashionable to the point of *de rigueur* to feel guilty that in some way, inevitably, you might be letting them down. It has become very PC to worry endlessly about whether everyone around you is happy all the time, as if somehow you have to put everyone else's happiness first.

CASE STUDY

Rose, forty, is a headmistress with three children under ten. She lives with Laurie, a musician.

I feel great guilt towards my friends. I don't see enough of them, I really don't. They have had to make do with my being very preoccupied and rather precious about my babies, and then with my being taken up by work and being tired. Most of them have just about hung on in there but there are some who have had enough.

I decided that the only way to really deal with it was to have dinner parties of twenty, four times a year. Only then could we manage to pay anyone back for the umpteen times they had had us round for dinner. The guilt has got slightly better since I have started doing that but only a bit. I am hoping that, as the kids grow up, it will disappear altogether.

I once told a confidante of mine how distressed I was leaving my youngest crying in nursery, when the day before he had been fine. 'I must be doing something wrong,' I wailed. 'I mean, he is too little

TOP TIP

Do a time budget: figure out whether you are actually living beyond your physical means as much as your financial ones.

to know that it's good going for me to be able to take him there at all at the moment.' My wise counsel said something along the lines of: 'It is very North London, this guilt, and this sense that avoiding misery is a goal. The point of life is, after all, to experience some disappointment and learn to cope. Even at a young age that's not a terrible thing.'

But today part of the drive to have great work–life balance is to make everything perfect – for everyone else. Be 'the best' boss. Be 'the best' colleague. Be 'the best' in bed. And of course be 'the best' friend, child, spouse... or mum. Commerce may have invented Mother's Day, Father's Day, and Valentine's Day, but each is a test of how guilt-free you can be on those days.

TOP TIP

Counteract 'I didn't do this' thoughts with 'yes, but I did do that'.

Shyama, divorced, works from home and has two daughters.

When I was married, it was all about being the best and having the best and knowing the best: what stress! Now I'm a single parent, I've had no choice but to cut back and the extraordinary thing is that, far from creating an even bigger imbalance, the fact that we're celebrating what we have, rather than mourning what we don't have, has created an equilibrium that has nothing to do with hours worked or bills received.

Resisting Temptation

Guilt, as we know, is fruitless. It is not only exhausting but it perpetuates the myth of perfection when the reality of 'good enough' might do instead.

It is essential not to feel guilty if you are on the See-Saw. Guilt is a saggy emotion, a wilting emotion, a Not Helpful feeling. Surround yourself with feisty people who know not to indulge in it. My friend Jane is a very good role model for this. She told me: 'I don't feel guilt. I'm not a good juggler. To use the ball analogy further, I'm not a good footballer, so I don't expect to score lots of goals. I don't mind dropping balls because I know I can pick them up again on a different occasion. So I don't give myself a hard time.'

 TOP TIP

Avoid toxic behaviour like moaning and bitching. It drains energy and is a way of getting at others – a sure sign than somewhere deep down you are getting at yourself.

Another friend, a single mother of two children, has had a number of serious operations. Alex is completely no-nonsense about the fact that this means her children are in day care a lot of the time. She says: 'I just get on with it and so do they. I would not dream of feeling guilty that I have to work the hours I do. I make sure that there is no self-pity around.'

Flora, forty-eight, an educational psychologist, lives with her mother who has Alzheimer's, along with her daughter, now aged thirteen, and her partner.

When we all moved in with mother in order to look after her, my daughter was only four and it was really hard trying to juggle the needs of my mum with the very different needs of a small child. There were so many complex sets of arrangements for care that it was quite overwhelming. I do feel guilty towards my daughter because quite a lot of the time her needs had to be forgotten as Mum's were more pressing. She missed out on some of the early social stuff because I really didn't have any space in my life for making play dates or hanging out with the other mothers. It meant that we felt a bit cut off from what always seemed to be happening very naturally with the other children and their mothers, and sometimes I felt sad about that.

It has made my daughter very independent and incredibly sociable as a teenager. She doesn't want to miss out on anything now.

Work Needs Me

The typical 'CrackBerry' addict who fiddles with emails at evenings and weekends is usually on a guilt trip. These have the net effect of

☞ TOP TIP

Never, ever be on email after 10 p.m. if you have trouble sleeping, and don't dabble at home with CrackBerry checking.

taking you further away from your family than a transatlantic flight does, which of course increases the guilt. It is a competitive jungle out there, and sometimes we overwork well into family time because we are anxious and upset about our work, and fear losing control. Whenever I find myself feeling guilty about work – usually in the form of 'I haven't done enough today' – I try to talk myself down from the dramatic ledge and think about the problem rationally.

Sometimes it isn't possible to get everything done. Sometimes a bit of leftover Fudge Brain from sleeplessness or a row at home can make you slack or less effective at work. Guilt isn't going to galvanize you in those moments and can only confirm your worst suspicion that you have failed.

Being Wrong

By the way, if you really are in the wrong, guilt can become your good conscience, but more often than not it is a way of getting stuck in a loop of low self-esteem. However, just in case, ask yourself whether what you are feeling is just that, a feeling, or whether something has happened

☞ TOP TIP

If feeling guilty is all about keeping you on the go, learn to be lazy sometimes, just to change gear. It is briefly uncomfortable, then a real relief.

that you have handled badly, or whether there is another reason to think you are in the wrong. Even then, you have to ask yourself whether the answer is to blame yourself or whether you have to just get beyond the moment.

Heather, a headhunter who works full time, writes freelance for several papers and teaches at City University Business School where she is a visiting professor. She is married with three sons .

Looking at my life, you would be forgiven for thinking I had no work–life balance. I manage a business full time and hold down two other jobs (writing and teaching) in my 'spare time'. And then I have three children and a husband to whom I have been married for twenty years. So how does anyone ever get enough of my attention? Surely everyone is short-changed, including me?

I have achieved many of the things I have sought to in my life and still feel that I enjoy good relationships with, and influence over, my family. Work–life balance is what you are happy with, not what someone else is impressed with. I have assessed what works for me and seek not to be influenced by what others think is the norm. So I don't bake cakes, or even pretend that I do, and I do send all three of my children to boarding school. This is not possible for everyone, emotionally or financially, but don't think it just removes the need for any personal input. My husband and children need just as many hours of my time put into their care and wellbeing as if I were with them – just given in a different way.

RECIPE

RECIPE: BATH KARAOKE

TIME: Ten minutes to half an hour.

INGREDIENTS: One tired mum; several tired children; bubble bath; lavender and geranium essential oil from Neal's Yard or similar; a shower attachment or, failing that, something resembling a microphone.

A very effective way to unwind is to belt out some songs with your kids at the end of a stressful day. It means you can get out of your work clothes, which marks the end of work and the beginning of home time. The aromatherapy guarantees a good vibe for all. Get one of the children to be the DJ and announce each 'singer' who can either belt out a favourite tune or, if you are me, make up an entirely silly 'I love you with your squidgy nose, yes I do' version.

Please note the single version of this or even the romantic version of this. In other words, this is a very versatile recipe indeed. The key ingredients of hot water, essential oil and at least one person willing to make a shower attachment into a microphone applies to all uses of Bath Karaoke. There is also a dry and fully clothed version: I particulary recommend unwiding in the Lucky Voice karaoke bar for a very long sing-song.

11

See-Saw Romance

This book is absolutely not about what Helen Fielding so memorably called 'Smug Marrieds' in *Bridget Jones's Diary*, not least because relationships, as we all know, take huge amounts of energy, effort, and that old T-word, Time, if they are to work or to last. Skipping on MQT (marital quality time) is a common failing as the divorce courts figures show, and if you are single or separated, making time for yourself is just as crucial, either to stop yourself being overwhelmed by wretchedness or to, yes, meet someone else. Even speed dating takes time, unless you speed date at home by video, in which case I fear that you have no life at all!

James Bond or Indiana Jones?

David Cameron and Gordon Brown were famously asked which heroic character they most identified with (Dave was 007 and Gordon was Indiana), but I want to ask them another question: are you a Planner or a Spur-of-the-Moment-er?

Political dividing lines may be one thing, but romantic tactics are another. For long-term couples it is pretty important to decide what kind of approach you take.

The spontaneous romancer seizes the moment she or he finds to grab a bite to eat together, cosy up on the sofa, send some flowers, or write a card, and, of course, make time for nookie. They might be more of a romantic but they might also be more lazy.

A girlfriend whose husband took leave of his senses and walked out on her after twenty-five years came to have lunch with me. As usual, I had Bag and Jewellery envy as she is always wonderfully put together even in her darkest moments. I particularly admired her bag.

(Incidentally, my top pecking order, wardrobe-wise, is probably (1) good jewellery (2) good handbag (3) good clothes and (4) good shoes in that order, because (1) and (2) always have to be top quality in my book, whereas (3) and (4) can be much less expensive as long as they are well chosen.)

But back to the bag. My friend looked over sadly at her beautifully stitched, red-leather patchwork quilt of a bag. 'He used to buy these for me,' she said. 'Now I've lost them, too.' What she was mourning was that spontaneous show of affection that is so crucial to romance. It doesn't have to involve spending money, or even the giving of presents. It can be an unexpected laugh together or holding hands in front of the telly ('Eurgh, snogging,' our children cry and wrinkle their noses in delighted disgust).

The Planner always books a babysitter on a Wednesday, and runs a romance schedule as if every month was a fertility chart, that is, leaving nothing to chance, because if it isn't scheduled, the thinking goes, it ain't going to happen.

There is much to be said for planning romance, although many people find it either impractical or a passion killer. We all know how crabby, miserable, failed, guilty, and lost we feel if romance stalls.

TOP TIP

Tell your loved one you love them and be generous to them. Never take your loved one for granted: they could do it to you and neither is right.

CASE STUDY

Sue, sixty-two, is a lawyer and reputation management consultant with two adult children and a first grandchild. She lives in London and in the Cotswolds.

As statistically about one in every three of us will divorce or separate, and many of us will do it more than once, I found it amazingly reassuring to discover just what enormous fun life could be as a singleton of advancing years, with just enough money to travel a little and be totally independent.

I personally recommend rather younger men – they have more energy, deal better with successful, financially secure women, and snore less!

See-Saw Singletons

See-Saw Singletons also divide into groups. There are the 'chance encounter' types, who want on the whole to be swept up in a sudden romance, and those who bring ambition into their search for lurve. These folk assiduously cultivate prospective partners through online dating or single-minded bar-propping at other people's weddings.

The advantage of singleton see-sawing these days is that the stigma of looking for partners has, as far as I can tell, been completely removed. I felt quite shocked when one of my closest girlfriends regaled me with stories of her hot telephone sex with a man she had met on the internet. In fact I was shocked to realize that this particular friend, and several others on the dating scene, had no problem at all meeting men and getting, shall we say, involved at a very early stage, only to move on to someone else pretty quickly because, as she put it, 'There is loads of choice out there.'

Of course, the stigma that remains associated with being single is the one about waiting too long to meet Mr Right and ending up childless. However, I know women in their twenties, thirties, and forties who now see being single as a fact of life to enjoy. These women enjoy having money, time, and freedom as well as the lack of a spouse to bicker with or compromise with. They know they might miss out having children and having a long-term snuggle companion, but they don't feel inferior for their choice or their circumstances.

This is important. Romance on the See-Saw happens best when you aren't desperate, but when you know who you are.

CASE STUDY

Tara, thirty-something, works in the media.

No matter what Richard Curtis tells you, the single life is rarely Bridget Jones, it is very likely you are not in a cool flat in Bermondsey.

You feel absurd because even though chums appear to be juggling pregnancy, a husband, a directorship and Feng Shui course they are in control. My job is not even nine to five and all I have in my fridge is a camembert and three cans of Red Bull. I haven't paid my council tax and last week, unintentionally, I stole a copy of the *Telegraph* from Marks and Spencer's: this gave me the tiniest of thrills.

If you're anything like me, you feel utter guilt for resenting a girlfriend who you thought you were seeing for a naughty lunchtime bottle of wine and she appears with small free-range child and suggests a smoothie in John Lewis. You smile and slip Marlboro Lights back into your handbag. On occasion, you have an amusing anecdote to tell chums then feel paranoid afterwards fearing they may think you are unstable / promiscuous / to be pitied / all of the above.

Second only to the 'No-Book, Book Club' is the 'No-Jog, Jogging Club'. The idea was simple: four girls living within a minute of Battersea Park, 2.7 miles circumference to run round, a view of the Thames, the Prince Charles peace pagoda for after-work serenity. Oh, what a joy. After to be rewarded with a white wine spritzer in a local bar, just the one: keep it healthy.

Following a couple of gos at this arrangement, a couple of us couldn't make the run but made 'the wine bit' after. This continued until all of us were only turning up for the spritzer followed by a bottle of Rioja. What is particularly delusional about this arrangement is the fact that we would turn up in jogging gear, less running from being single, more jogging for freedom.

Trick or Treat

My friend Annabelle always grumbles that her husband insists on staying somewhere really expensive when they go away, when in fact all she wants is to stay somewhere modest and have a low-key time with her man. 'I can't understand why he always makes such a big deal of it,' she

☞ TOP TIP

Make sure you do get special time alone together with your partner. This means going away alone, despite the cost and the childcare headache, at least twice a year for a long weekend.

says, 'because apart from anything else it sets up such high expectations.'

Sue gets exasperated because her bloke can't be bothered to lift himself off the sofa in the evenings, and she takes this as a sign of great neglect, almost hostility. 'It's not that I want some special romance every night, but a little attention would be good.'

CASE STUDY

Polly, forty-four, is a service manager for a charity and has three teenage children. She has been with her Italian partner, Marco, for twenty-one years.

It's really hard to give your relationships quality time, but I'm in the stage where the children are moving off and our eldest is about to go to university. I am aware that there has to be something to fill the conversation, which is now all about the children: what is happening, where are they and what are they doing.

I know that we will have to re-establish our relationship a bit more, particularly as we work so well together as parents. We will both have to remember the things that connected us twenty years ago, before we had the children, and find things that we enjoy doing together.

Mood Swing

 TOP TIP

Put your considerable talent, energy and sex appeal into showing the one you love... lurve.

The sex See-Saw is well known to swing down far too much for most people's liking. The sparkly, bodily, bonding bit of romance is what everyone wants and worries about when it dips below a certain level. Separating out sex from romance is important. It is OK on occasion to not be in the mood for one or the other, but it obviously isn't OK for most couples to fail to make time for them or lose the inclination altogether over long periods.

CASE STUDY

Ruth, forty-five, a nurse, is married to Terry, a taxi driver. They have three kids, aged seven, ten and fourteen.

Terry used to come to bed all up for it when in all honesty he had barely seemed to notice me, perhaps had even been a bit short with me, but had definitely not touched me all day long. I told him that he would have to make a bit more of an effort than that, that if he was attentive to me and made me feel a bit special, who knows, I might actually be in the mood. I would certainly entertain the idea rather than feeling like the invisible woman all evening until he got to bed and suddenly was all over me.

He has learned from that actually. Well, I've made it worth his while, haven't I?

How you rekindle romance, or stay kindled, is very much a personal thing, of course, but everyone seems to agree on some basic rules:

1. Make time to be alone together regularly.
2. If you are bored by your routine, try to vary it.
3. Get away on your own together without the children.

CASE STUDY

Annabelle, a mother of three children, is a freelance consultant in the social sector.

We have found that making time for ourselves is vital, as a weekend without the kids – or just an evening out of the house – provides a huge boost as well as a reminder about what it is that we are passionate about ourselves.

There is of course also the big S-question. I know that I am not alone in having experienced a big drop in my libido after having kids. I have found that just doing it, even when not at all in the mood at first, does work, and usually I do get into it... Even when the thought does not appeal, the act tends to get me going. If we go too long without sharing such physical intimacy, I find that we can get more and more distant from each other and end up cohabiting, living alongside one another, as opposed to really together. And tempers rise much more quickly. So my advice is: *just do it!*

The other problem about relationships is the descent into the pettiness of daily life, the 'Why have you not emptied the dustbin?'

question. As with children, I think you need to choose which fights to pick. It is not actually that important who empties the dustbin. What is important is that my husband shows me love and respect. If he chooses not to do so by emptying the dustbin, I have learned to let go. Otherwise, a spiral of small squabbles and resentments build up and you realize that you have become like every other couple that you have always despised – bickering about the minutiae of everyday life.

Annual Leave

Opinion is divided about whether you need to blow your wages on saucy knickers in Agent Provocateur in order to have a truly good time, but I do know this: time on your own with your lover or significant other but without the children is a staple ingredient to good See-Saw living. At least twice a year you have to strive with every fibre to go away together for three nights at least. It is so hard to summon the discipline to do this, not least because it usually involves stressfully large amounts of organization and money.

We took some time on our wedding anniversary one year and sent the children to stay with my parents while we... stayed at home. My mum was rather disappointed that we were not leaping on a plane to go somewhere exotic, but to be honest, having the house to ourselves, and our home city of London to explore, was just lovely. We went out to the Lea Valley on a beautiful sunny day and walked around the butterfly meadows, came home, and had a fabulous curry.

It is true that this is the very time our eldest managed to cut his

TOP TIP

Remember that affairs almost always end in tears and sick: avoid, avoid, avoid.

head open in the school playground, and my 90-year old father ended up taking him to A&E for stitches. Even so we kept guilt at bay. 'Mum, don't panic!' said Roman when he rang to tell us.

So, start currying favour with whoever is most likely to get you some getaway time.

CASE STUDY

Shyama, divorced, works from home and has two daughters.
The joy of being divorced is that every other weekend I'm childfree. Initially this was unbearable, but over the years I've come to appreciate those four days a month. It's me-time. Some weekends I have wall-to-wall social engagements. On others, I do absolutely nothing. It's fantastic. I think now that if my ex and I had each had a weekend a month where we were childfree and did our own individual things, we'd still be together.

On the See-Saw: Linda

Linda is a broadcaster and columnist.

Work–life balance? I've got the worry–life balance now. But also a few friends.

When I was ITN's Scotland correspondent, I had impressive control over the news agenda. If I happened to sip too much wine (just a little, I was no Merlot lout), major stories broke. When I remained sober, the Scottish scene was tranquil.

For six years I lived on a pager, awaiting the next instruction from the London news desk. Journalistically, I was 'it' in Scotland. I covered the whole of that heather-clad 'hood, alongside a couple of cameramen who did the twiddly bits. Back then, there was just work, no other life. On a rare day off, I landed back in my flat and said (to myself, obviously): 'Oh dear. Nothing arranged. Which is just as well, as I've no one to do it with.' Whereupon I was perversely glad when the pager went, thereby saving me from confronting the fact that I'd had surgery on my social life.

The chirrup of that pager accompanied me everywhere, auguring my dispatch to an unfolding event. News always broke at a lower temperature; I spent years earnestly enunciating the facts of a tragedy on News at Ten *whilst blue with cold beside a house fire. Or on a mountain. Or beside the sea.*

Friends were used to my meek phone call, typically made from Peterhead harbour with my hair smelling of cod (OK, they didn't know that bit).

'Sorry, I've got to—'

'Let me guess... cancel. What is it this time? Capsized trawler?'

'No, the EU has tightened the quotas on cod and I'm doing vox pops tomorrow at the fish market.' (Which, incidentally, started at 4 a.m. and

161

was staffed by men in white wellies who, I swear, were half human, half haddock.)

So I left ITN after six years, seeking the chance to spend time with any friends I could persuade to remember me. And how is freelance life? Well, I no longer strive for a work-life balance, but a worry-life balance. The chirrup of the pager has been replaced by a warning bell in my head, which tolls to bring attention to my fears. Like, where is the next job coming from? Am I a direct debit away from destitution? Will I end up drinking meths from a shoe in my old age?

But the friends are back. And the Merlot tastes better, knowing I won't be nursing a hangover beside a gaping cod at 4 a.m. Never drink red wine with fish, I say.

Afterword

Does my sassiness upset you?
Why are you beset with gloom?
'Cause I walk like I've got oil wells
Pumping in my living room.

Just like moons and like suns,
With the certainty of tides,
Just like hopes springing high,
Still I'll rise.

'Still I Rise', Maya Angelou

When I told my family and friends I was writing a book about work–life balance, they laughed or gasped with incredulity. 'Er... and you have the time?' was about the most subdued comment. A sudden panic set in, the kind of awful penny-dropping when you have done something rash and have been found out. 'That's beyond hilarious,' said one friend, a point that was repeated by others in a weird chorus. 'What do you mean?' I said defensively, remembering my mad dance to get out of the house on time, or to complete a document by morning, or be back home for bedtime, or visit my unwell friend, or any number of efforts that have clearly been lost on everyone except me. Perception is, after all, about reality. 'Well,' they said, breaking the news to me gently, 'you have tons of energy. But do you have work–life balance?

That would have to be a no.'

I can argue it both ways, depending on what kind of crazy day I've had, or whether I can say all the children seem calm and happy at any given point, or whether there are more clients on the list at the end of the month than at the beginning – and happy staff too. But I know that one thing life isn't about these days for any of us is predictability or even stability. We go up and down on some kind of See-Saw whether we like it or not. This book has, I hope, shown that even if you do feel like this, you are not alone.

In the BF (Before Family) years, in my first big job as a publicist for the publishers Virago in the late 1980s, I was given the legendary American poet and civil rights activist Maya Angelou as 'my' author to promote when her fifth volume of autobiography was published. This was less like work and more like Very Heaven. I toured around the UK by train one glorious summer with Dr Angelou and her entourage to book signings and publicity events that involved picnic hampers, tots of whisky, and some of the best company I have ever enjoyed.

If this was work, I wanted to do it for ever. I had no children then, so I had time *and* no guilt. As time went by I started a business and begun a family life. I'm no longer carefree I have obligations to others besides myself, managing priorities and time has become as essential as managing money. But I am lucky to have stayed in love with my work for twenty-five years (not something to take for granted by any means). *Not* loving what you do does definitely make life on the See-Saw much, much harder. Can you possibly change your job? Retrain, redefine what you do? Is it at least worth having this as a goal?

Sassiness

Maya Angelou's inspiring life story really is one of overcoming adversity with aplomb, energy, and, as she puts it so well, sassiness. We don't feel lucky in our work, our loves and lives all of the time. In fact, much of our time is spent on a treadmill of obligations, no matter how enjoyable or indispensable they are.

Today's working generation may not always walk as if we have oil wells pumping in our living rooms but we have feminism pumping in our veins, with more freedom and economic power than at any time in history – despite the gender pay gap. Yet even though we 'won' the right to do it all, guess what? It doesn't feel easy or particularly right.

Men feel, despite the pay gap, that in many ways they have 'lost' something to women's 'gain' in the world of work. They still have to work; they can't take time off to have babies; and maybe, just maybe, they have a point about being 'passed over' by women who still take most of the credit for childcare, even when a good many men are now house husbands or do their fair share of childcare. In reality everyone feels confused, short-changed, and, yes, short-tempered. In reality it seems as if we spend more time on the See-Saw than we do on the beach, as if it is winter with the dark closing in early all year long when we have to work, work, work (or worse, fear for our jobs).

Light in the Tunnel

So this book aimed to throw some light on some of the dark corners of gloom in our lives that we all see around us at least some of the time, and offer advice on how to cope. I cheated by asking a group of wonderful, wise women and men of many different ages, life stages, and experiences, to join me in putting together our top tips for coping with, among others, the pressures of:

- developing a career and family at the same time
- managing childcare (I can hear you groan)

- finding time for yourself (I can hear you laugh)
- finding time for your Significant Other (I hear you wince in shame at the neglect of your precious person)

And, of course, we all want to be Fulfilled all the time with a capital F, but avoid Guilt with a capital G. We want to do our feminist forebears proud – at least I do – so that we not only need to keep fighting the good fight for women to get equal rights and equal pay in the workplace, but we also want to look fabulous and deploy our multitasking skills to the max without feeling that our gain is somehow men's loss. Men want to bond with their children in a completely different way from most of their fathers' generations, while also being less enslaved to work and more fulfilled. This isn't a narrow middle class dream. The ads on TV are all consistently selling one thing: freedom, flexibility, and a good family life.

On life's See-Saw, you are only ever going up one way or down the other, but with a bit of technique, timing, and tenacity thrown in among, of course, whatever luck comes your way, you can also stay in the middle more than you think. You may already be using recipes for success and survival without even crediting yourself. You should stop beating yourself up that you are less able to manage than others, or could do more 'if only' this or that, and instead take heart that you can learn some good ways of managing an increasing number of pressures on your time, your finances, and your expectations.

I was looking for, and found, evidence that reassured me that women and men are coming up with different ways of managing this frantic, post-feminist world, in which we somehow asked for – and got – the right to work hard, play hard, and family hard, all at once.

The springy tone of Maya Angelou's poem 'Still I Rise' is the one I wanted to capture in this book – the moment when you are down, when your See-Saw hits the bottom, but you just put a spring in your step… and rise right back up.

Acknowledgements

To Alaric and the children, Rachael, Max, Roman, Anoushka and Wolfgang Jim, without whom...

Particular credit and thanks goes to Sophie Radice for her case study research and to Nicola Streeten for her beautiful illustrations: www.nicolastreeten.com

My parents Eric and Marlene have been invaluable as the unit known as 'GrandmaGrandpa'.

Thanks to my colleagues and clients at Editorial Intelligence for being both interested in, and supportive of, this string to my bow.

Amy Silverton did heroic work untangling the spaghetti that is See-Saw law. Lennie Goodings and Margaret Bluman spurred me on early on, as did Jessica Morris, Ruth McCall, Nina Planck, Julia Llewellyn Smith, Marion McGilvary, Dorothy Schwarz, Saskia Sissons, and Liz de Planta, Alice Sherwood and my sister-cousins Habie and Tanya.

Finally thanks to the following for variations on a theme of friendship, contributions, and / or pearls of wisdom which have made it in some shape or form to this book: Alice Belibi, Sarah Benton, Tim Blackford, Franc Bettilot, Jane Brien, Janice Browning, Richard Carvalho, Ginger Cockerham, James Caplin, Smarayda Christioforou, Sally Cramer, Finn Craig, Antonia Cox, Linda Cullen, Sarah Dunning, Liesel Evans, David Farnsworth, Jonathan Farewell, Jenny Fitzpatrick, Christina Flowers, Jenny Flowers, Sol Freedman, Amanda Fone, Clare Furey, Flora Golding, Marie Gomez, Rose Grantham, Alan Harcard, Tara Hamilton-Miller, Laura Hewitt, Betina Kaplovsky, Linda Kennedy, Gemma Lines, Heather McGregor, Phil and Anne Meadowcroft, Julia Neuberger, Shyama Perera, Adele Radice, Jane Rathbone, Avril Robson, Alex Sandberg, Ruth Shipton, Mary Ann Sieghart, Anya Schiffrin, Shirley Soskin, Sue Stapely, Polly Stringer, Suzanna Taverne, Sally Tedstone, Nina Temple, David Watson, Anna Wilson, Deborah Wilson, Ginny Withers, Phillipa Woodham and Ian Wylie.

And to everyone at Atlantic, especially Toby Mundy, Karen Duffy and Sarah Norman. All are incomparable.

I offer the usual disclaimers that all errors and silliness are mine and mine alone. Everyone did their best to steer me clear of the worst of them.